BELLS OF SHANGRI-LA

BELLS OF SHANGRI-LA

Scholars, Spies, Invaders in Tibet

PARIMAL BHATTACHARYA

SPEAKING TIGER

SPEAKING TIGER PUBLISHING PVT. LTD
4381/4, Ansari Road, Daryaganj
New Delhi 110002

First published in India by Speaking Tiger 2019

ISBN: 978-93-88326-92-6
eISBN: 978-93-88326-93-3

10 9 8 7 6 5 4 3 2 1

'It is so hard to tell where the real ends and
the dreams begin.'

—Lila Majumdar,
The Yellow Bird's Feather

Contents

A MIRAGE

AT SHANGRI-LA'S DOOR

THE YAK BELL'S CHIME

THE BLUE BOOK

'It was this question that we were resolved to answer. We would, if possible, go right through the gorge, and tear this last secret from its heart.'

—Frank Kingdon Ward,
The Riddle of the Tsangpo Gorges

The Mall

From Scandal Point, where a maharaja is said to have eloped with a viceroy's daughter—or was it his wife?—keeping the Ridge on the left, one could walk down the Mall Road and pass Ta-Tung & Co., Kumar, Rama and Company, Ramchand Bishandas, Shyamlal & Sons, Gaindamal Hemraj—the row of once-famous shops where the aura of a lost time still lingers. From the second half of the 19th century until Independence, Shimla, then Simla, was the summer capital of British India. Top officers and their families promenaded on this stretch of road, these shops decked up with fancy merchandise to charm them. From the choicest silk to premium wines, from perfumes to musical instruments, all accessories of fine living were to be found here. There were watchmakers, gun-sellers, shoe-makers, photography studios, barbershops, haberdashers, piano-tuners and saddlers—most of these establishments were run by Europeans. There was also a large pavilion where every year, at the onset of summer, carpet-sellers from Lahore set up stalls. Silk-weavers from the Kangra Valley arrived with mule caravans and remained until Diwali, when the last narrow-gauge railway trains filled with sahib-mems left the hill station.

Gone are those days. After Partition, the men from Lahore have stopped coming, the perfumeries and haberdashers have folded up, the piano-tuners and saddlers have lost their calling. The Chinese shoe-makers have stayed back, but many Muslim-owned shops have changed hands. Some have changed identity but not the name; the old signboards have remained but the wares have changed. Some have resisted change. They cling on like the leathery old men around town who lounge on concrete benches at the Ridge, walking sticks resting between the knees, their cold, rheumy eyes turned to the tides of time. In the last two decades, this famous road's grey colonial heritage has been gilded with the shine of a new economy. Barista, Adidas, Benetton, Domino's and others have cast their familiar glow-signs to trap the shoals of tourists that pass by. They come from all corners of the country. As they tramp up from the taxi-stand below and walk down this street, a perceptible spring sets into their gait. Is it because their legs hit a stretch of level ground after the tiring climb? Or is it because of a euphoria that goes off in the subconscious mind as one enters a once-forbidden zone? Natives weren't allowed on Mall Road in the colonial era. At Scandal Point, under the slate-roofed traffic umbrella, a policeman with peaked red cap and white gloves stands like a ghost from those times.

And here, bedazzled by the shop windows, the logos of well-known brands and glossy mannequins, the eye can easily pass over the dull signboard of an antique bookstore. Its smoke-blue door, the old books on Tantra and Mughal miniatures displayed behind glass give the shop the appearance of a faded watercolour. As one pushes open the door, a bell tinkles overhead. The eye takes a few seconds to adjust to the dimness before it discerns mountains of books lining the walls, heaped on tables and most of the floor. A handsome old gentleman with a trimmed grey beard is seen at the far end of the room, hunched over a table under a lamp with a conical shade; he is peering through silver-rimmed glasses at a very old map. A grey cat occupies a corner of the table, its eyes closed, its back arched like a tea cosy under the warm light of the lamp.

The cat opens an eye at the bell's chime, inspects the stranger cursorily, and turns its gaze to a yellow moth gyrating in the shaft of light. The man, presumably the owner of the shop, never looks up.

Situated on the busy Mall Road, the shop attracts curious onlookers; very few of them turn out to be customers. Most slip out after a quick glance at the pile of dusty old books, some browse for a while; still others, who come here after reading about this establishment in guide books, enquire the price of a rare first edition. How much of this bookstore's fame rests on its rare collection, and how much on the fancy price tags, is a matter of conjecture; but its clientele are mostly Western tourists. A quick look across the shelves reinforces this fact: Buddhism, Indian classical music, illustrated *Kamasutra*s, coffee-table books on the interiors of the palaces of native maharajas, Company paintings and handicrafts, colonial anthropology, memoirs of British civil servants and other assorted subjects that can be conveniently packed into the amorphous holdall called Indology. Most of these books were salvaged from rundown family collections and private libraries in and around Shimla. For more than a century, this town bore witness to the history of a vast subcontinent, countless officials and men of letters flocked here for work and play. Carriage-loads of printed matter followed them here and were left behind. The bookshop also has its searching net cast across all the major cities of India.

The yellow moth fluttered in the musty air; the cat on the table shut its eyes; a Tibetan mask gazed with fierce eyes from a stool in a corner of the room. I strayed inside the shop, browsing the faded lettering on the spines of old leather-bound books, into the womb of a delicate, stilled time. *Spectator 1882-92*, *The Bible*, *Collected Poems of Oliver Goldsmith*, *From the Caves and Jungles of Hindoostan*, *The Art of Nicholas Roerich*... A pot-pourri of subjects, bound by a single thread of time; the books, the furniture, the prints, the shopkeeper, and even the cat appeared to be older than independent India. *Indian Police... Journal... Magic & Mystery in Tibet ... The Nabobs... Kalachakra Tantra... Curry & Rice... Vignettes... The Way to Shambhala... Csoma de Koros...* My eyes flitted past, until they came to rest on a word: *Kinthup*.

Kinthup! A bell tinkled somewhere inside my head, a door was pushed open a little.

But this was not exactly a book. It was a typed document—in royal size, bound in blue felt, and a seal of the Survey of India, with a map of the country in a circle and the imperial crown on top, embossed on the cover. On the title page was printed:

Report of Pandit Kinthup's Exploration of Yarlung Tsangpo
As narrated before the Hon'ble Members of
the Tibet Frontier Commission, 25-28 March 1914
With a Note on the Vindication of Kinthup by Captain G.F.T. Oakes, R.E.
Office of the Foreign Secretary, Government of India
Summer Hill, Simla
1914

As I picked up the weighty volume and held it, I felt a quickening in my veins. I had laid my hands on this document many years ago, in another hill town.

A long violent political agitation had just ended in Darjeeling, life was limping back to normal. A pile of fire-damaged books and papers had found their way to a kabari shop below the Mahakal market. I had found the volume, damp and ash-spotted, in the pile. It was a very old document, printed in 1886 or thereabouts, on a subject that was uncannily similar: it was a report on the explorations of a few spies in the Tibet region. Among them was the adventure of a man named Kinthup, codenamed K.P., who had gone off in search of the mystery of the river Tsangpo. I had begun to devour it right there, standing inside the cramped shop, amid stacks of old tattered books, as a dim foggy day bled into evening outside.

'You can take it home if it's of any value to you, Sir,' Nima Tashi, the shopkeeper, had said. 'You needn't pay anything.'

I was a regular at Nima Tashi's kabari shop; it was home to the old paperbacks left behind by tourists in hotel rooms and coffee shops. Most were crappy novels and wellness books, but sometimes unexpected gems did turn up. I paid 20 rupees—the price printed on the cover was 1 rupee 4 annas—for that soggy, crumbling slab of paper and took it home. Within a few days, dark violet fungi appeared on the pages and stuck them together. But the tale of Kinthup lingered in my memory for a long time, linked with the memory of an acrid fungal smell, until it was lost in the morass of other tales. The document, too, was lost. My housekeeper had probably used it along with old newspapers to light a brazier and dry washings on a wet monsoon day.

Now, as I held the blue felt-bound typescript in my hand in that bookshop in Shimla, Kinthup's tale returned to me, and the memory of that cloying smell, the fog of a lost time slipped in through a crack in the door. I walked up to the shop-owner and asked its price. The gentleman came around the table and took the large volume in his hands.

'Eighteen thousand and five hundred only,' he said in a low, silky voice.

'Eighteen thou...!' My jaw dropped.

'Yes, in Indian currency. The price in dollars would come to around 25,000 rupees. This is one of the two existing copies of a once-classified document, the only one in India; the other one is in the India Office Library in London.'

He spoke in a slightly accented English, a glint of amusement playing in his eyes behind the silver-rimmed glasses.

I protested. 'The only copy? But I have seen this in printed form, in a second-hand shop in Darjeeling.'

'Oh yes, I know.' The man nodded his head. 'But not this one. Wait...'

He handed me the document and entered a narrow gully between the shelves, wagging his index finger like the tail of a dog searching for a bone, picked up a large printed volume and returned.

'This, you must have seen this.'

Memories rushed back as I laid my eyes on it: yes, this one. But this was a better preserved copy—a report on the explorations of five explorers in Sikkim, Bhutan and Nepal; Kinthup was one of them. It had been published in 1889, by Colonel H.R. Thuillier, then the Surveyor General of India, and printed at the office of the Trigonometrical Branch in Dehradun.

'Pundit Kinthup went to Tibet in 1880, the British government sent him. It took him four years to complete the mission, and this report was compiled soon after his return,' the gentleman said, tapping the volume. 'Thirty years later, when the McMahon

Line was being drawn, Kinthup was summoned here, to Shimla, and was debriefed again. This one was based on that session.' He pointed to the copy I was holding. 'But if you wish to buy this printed copy, I can give it at a discounted price.'

I handed the blue felt-bound typescript back to him without a word. He moved his hand caressingly over its cover and put both the volumes together back into the shelf.

In 1880, when Kinthup was sent to explore the unknown course of the Tsangpo, Tibet was a land of mystery that lay across the great mountains of the Himalaya. The mystery cast a veil over its forbidding geography and the people who lived there. By that time almost the entire Indian subcontinent had come under British rule, there was hardly any region left to be explored. But Tibet had continued to remain a blank spot on the map, a rather big spot, twenty times the size of England. For the adventurers of the Raj, there was the call of the unknown. But above this was a pang of anxiety. Across Tibet lay mighty Russia and its imperial designs. A thorough knowledge of this land on the roof of the earth was thus a matter of diplomatic necessity for the men who ruled India.

It was a matter of economic necessity as well. Since ancient times, trade routes had connected Tibet with the Gangetic plains through high mountain passes. Silk, metal, ivory, salt and foodgrains were exported from India in exchange for wool, butter, leather and yak tails. This had continued during British rule, and new items like glass, indigo and cutlery had been added to the list of goods bartered. Warren Hastings, the astute Governor General in the late 18th century, had realized the importance of this trade link and had sent a diplomatic mission to Tibet. It was successful. The East India Company became friends with the Panchen Lama, the priest-king of western Tibet. But Hasting's successors didn't follow up on this friendship; rather, they became embroiled in the bickering between Nepal, Sikkim and Bhutan. With two big foreign powers, Russia and Britain, breathing down its neck, Tibet closed its doors to outsiders and tightly secured the mountain passes that led to it. It became nearly impossible for Indians from the plains, let alone white-skinned Europeans, to enter the mountain kingdom.

Tibetans and other local hill tribes monopolized trade along the high-altitude routes that remained snow-bound for most of the year. The only other people who had access to them were Buddhist monks. It was relatively easy for scholars and mendicant monks to cross the passes and find shelter in the Tibetan villages, a tradition that had been going on for hundreds of years. The British began to exploit this chink. Spies disguised as monks were sent to Tibet. They were called Pundits.

The Pundits were drafted from among the hill people. They were trained in techniques of topographic survey and given instruments specially manufactured for this purpose: sextants and theodolites that could be hidden in the secret chambers of boxes, compasses fitted on walking staffs, papers and pencils tucked inside hollowed prayer wheels. Their rosaries had one hundred beads instead of the usual one hundred and eight, to measure distances by keeping count of their paces. Sometimes it was risky to even carry papers, and they were required to cast the survey data into rhymed stanzas and commit them to memory. This way, from the notes and narrations of these Pundit-spies, lines and shades began to appear on the blank spot in the maps, above the creased mantle of the Himalaya.

But one mystery remained: What was the exact shape of a river? This river has its origin at 24,000 feet in the Tsang province in western Tibet, which gave it the name Tsangpo. It takes an easterly course along one of the innumerable parallel folds in the Himalayan mountain ranges that appear on maps like dense creases, but in reality are some of the deepest gorges on the planet. Running east for about a thousand miles, Tsangpo enters an impenetrable canyon to vanish into the labyrinth of knotted mountains and, within a span of 200 miles, plunges 9,000 feet, takes a sharp turn to the south and debouches into the plains of India. It is then known as Dihang and Brahmaputra. No other river in the world descends so dizzyingly steep a gradient with such an immense volume of water.

For a long time, geographers debated whether Tsangpo and Brahmaputra were one and the same river. Some argued that Tsangpo flowed east into Burma and became Irrawaddy. There were others who claimed that the river Subansiri connected Tsangpo with Brahmaputra. Two other major rivers in this region, Dibang and Lohit, complicated the matter. No less confusing was the fact that the same river is called by different names on its long journey from Tibet into India: Tsangpo, Yarlung Tsangpo, Dihang, Siang, Burha-Luit and Brahmaputra. James Rennel, the first Surveyor General of India, had guessed as early as 1765 that Tsangpo was Brahmaputra. But the forbidding topography, the politically sensitive frontier and the war-like tribes who inhabited this region had made it impossible to find proof. The few attempts that were made on the upstream of Dihang to seek out its headwaters had ended in failure. Nobody had any doubt that a white-skinned Westerner was not fit for this mission; his physical features would be a dead giveaway.

Who, then?

In the 1870s, Darjeeling was a fledgling hill station that had been attracting workers and artisans from the villages of Sikkim and Nepal. A Lepcha man from Sikkim had come there, borne on this tide of migration. He was short, sturdy, around thirty years old, and his name was Kinthup. Kinthup did odd jobs in town until he found work as a tailor in the bazaar. Around this time the Survey of India set up an office in Darjeeling and began to send Pundits on clandestine missions into Tibet. Kinthup was picked up as an assistant of one Nem Singh, code-named G.M.N., on an exploration of the course of Tsangpo. The mission did not yield anything, but on that assignment Kinthup displayed the three essential virtues of a secret explorer: intelligence, physical stamina and trustworthiness. Lt. Henry Harman had then joined as the chief of the survey office in Darjeeling. He was not a desk-bound officer, and he had a special interest in the riddle of the Tsangpo-Brahmaputra. It was Harman who sent Kinthup on another mission to explore the great river.

A requisite for promotion in service had forced me to join a three-week refresher course in the Academic Staff College in Shimla. The College was on Summer Hill, away from the bustle of the town, inside the leafy campus of Himachal University. A few steps away was the Viceregal Lodge, a fairy-tale palace of grey sandstone on a flattened hilltop, and a tiny railway station a few hundred feet below. The guest-house where I was staying stood on a rise above the station. Every day, two pairs of narrow-gauge trains stopped on their way to Shimla and back to the hot plains; nobody got in or out. On a weekday morning, shuttle buses from around the town would ferry in students, making the campus come alive with noise and colours, but by mid-afternoon the crowd would ebb. Summer Hill would grow deserted like an empty bird's nest; one would hear the breeze in the tall deodars.

Endless lecture sessions would go on, every work-day, inside the staff college. Late in the afternoon, a few of us would slip away like boarding-school boys and trek into town to soak up the gay atmosphere on Mall Road. After I chanced upon the blue, felt-bound document in that bookshop, I began to sneak out alone.

From Summer Hill, an oak-lined avenue wound its way along the western flank of the wooded mountain to the Ridge. It was September, the long season of rains was drawing to a close. Before dusk, the sun would slip behind the Pir Panjal range, turning the sky into liquid emerald and gold, setting the casements of the magnificent colonial-era buildings on fire. I'd make my way through the press of tourists, scrambling to photograph themselves in that magical light. A page in a story would haunt my thoughts, a story whose spell was drawing me, my nerves sharpened with suspicion: would I still find the blue book?

I would push open the smoke-blue door. The bell would ring. The cat would open an eye. Wreaths of vapour would rise from a cup of black coffee into the column of light.

Sometimes I wouldn't find the gentleman at his seat. A maroon jacket would hang around the chair's upholstered back. Behind it, upon the window panes, the parallel curves of distant ranges would be suspended in pellucid mist like a Japanese watercolour. He'd suddenly appear from behind a bookshelf or climb down a stepladder—absent-minded, a pen and a notepad in his hand. A diabolic plot would sweep through my head: what if I dropped a narcoleptic pill in his coffee mug, rushed out with the blue book, got it photocopied in the bazaar below and put it back in the shelf before he came to?

The thought would make me giddy as I'd stand there with the document open in my hands. The Tibetan mask would glower at me from upon the stool. One day I found that the mask had gone up on the shelf, the stool was empty. As I went to sit on it, the gentleman glanced at me briefly from over the spectacles. I couldn't discern any change of expression on the bearded face.

There Was a River

When Kinthup was being trained for the Tsangpo mission, a Chinese lama was staying in Darjeeling. He had a passport to Tibet. Moreover, he could read and write; Kinthup was illiterate. So it was decided that Kinthup would go into Tibet disguised as the lama's servant. The Chinese passport would give them free access there, the lama would also assist Kinthup to keep the survey records.

Though he couldn't read and write, Kinthup had mastered the basic skills of topographic survey and the working of instruments. He also had an amazing memory. The two men set out from Darjeeling on a wet afternoon in July 1880. Kinthup was leaving behind his wife, two young sons and a newborn daughter in a tiny shack in Butcher Bustee. The code of espionage forbade him to share with anyone the details of his mission, which was expected to be completed in four months. Accordingly, the government had disbursed a small sum for the upkeep of his family during this period. Kinthup and the lama were given a purse of 100 rupees and some silver pieces that could be exchanged for currency. The plan was that they would reach Gyala, a village near the western end of the Tsangpo gorge, up to which the earlier mission of Nem Singh had been able to reach, and from there press on into the gorge.

They entered Tibet from Sikkim through the Donkia Pass and halted by the lake Cholamo for a couple of days, to follow the caravan of traders from Gyantse who'd come here to exchange goods with their Sikkimese counterparts. The two went to Lhasa, stopped at Sera monastery, where the lama spent a few days feasting with old friends. From here on they took on the disguise of mendicant monks and continued to travel by begging for food and halting at jikkiyops—travellers' sheds erected by the Tibetan government to protect wayfarers from inclement weather and wild animals. Sometimes they spent the nights in caves. The rough life took its toll on the lama's health, and they had to halt at a place for three weeks for him to recuperate. As the route grew difficult—with the mountains rising higher and closing in from all sides, the forests growing denser and trackless—a mean and choleric man emerged from the shell of the monk; he began to abuse Kinthup like some do servants. It took them three months to reach Gyala, a settlement of half a dozen houses by the river and the ruins of a monastery nearby. It was November, the river was low. They crossed it and pressed on along the western bank on a path that grew more difficult at every step. Three days later they came to Pemakochung. But Kinthup couldn't find a path that was close to the river as it forced its way into the heart of the canyon. They were forced to retrace their steps and follow a path that went around this section, bent back and rejoined the Tsangpo further downstream.

By now the lama was at his wit's end. He had imagined the expedition to be a carefree picnic at the expense of the British government. This was too much for him. He continued to ill treat Kinthup. In the village of Thun Tsung, he fell for the charms of a woman from the Lopa tribe, the headman's wife, and they stopped there for four months. By the time the two men reached the dzong of Tongkyuk, their purse had dwindled.

Here the lama became suspiciously friendly with the dzongpon, the castle chief, and they were given food and shelter in the servants' quarters.

After two days' rest at the dzong, the lama said to Kinthup: 'My soul is burning with desire for that Lopa woman. I must go and see her again for one last time. Don't worry, I'll return in a few days.'

That night, one of dzongpon's servants entered Kinthup's room and, without a word, began to rummage through his belongings. He was a thickset man with long hair bound in a topknot and piercing eyes. But he appeared to be completely deaf as Kinthup's loud protests failed to move him. To stop him, Kinthup lunged forward and grabbed him by the waist. The very next moment he found himself lifted off the ground by an animal force and flung upon the stone floor. The man towered above, snorting in anger, with a bare foot raised inches above Kinthup's face, ready to squash it. The big toe on the foot was missing. With surprising confidence, the man now fished out a pistol and a compass from a secret pocket of the canvas sack that had eluded even the guards of Lhasa.

'Don't!' Kinthup pleaded, still sprawled on the floor. 'These belong to my government.'

'Shut your mouth or I'll shove my foot into it!' the man said, speaking in a curiously quiet voice. 'These will be returned when that lama comes back.'

Kinthup was shifted from the servants' quarters to a corner of the stable, where he was given the job of cutting grass for the dzongpon's horses. When it was found out that he could sew clothes, he was given the task of making quilt jackets for the dzongpon and his sons. Days passed, Kinthup waited for the lama's return. He earned his two meagre meals by sewing clothes and doing other odd jobs. His drudgery continued for two months. A full year had elapsed since he had set out from Darjeeling, a large part of the Tsangpo's course still remained to be charted.

One day, Kinthup went to the dzongpon. 'I don't know when my master will return, but I must leave now,' he said. 'Please give me back the pistol and the compass.'

'Leave? Where to?' The dzongpon laughed, showing tobacco-stained teeth. 'Neither will your master return, nor will you ever leave!'

'What do you mean?' Kinthup asked, shocked.

'That damned lama has sold you for 50 rupees and gone back to China. I'm your master now!'

Kinthup was now sent to the dzongpon's village, a day's march from Tongkyuk and perched on a cliff above a stream, to do the duties of a common slave. He was given a place to sleep in the sheepfold, among the animals, on the edge of a plot of barley. Above it, over thick stands of juniper and rhododendron, rose the snow-capped mountains. The stream, a tributary of the Tsangpo, flowed over rapids at a drop of a few hundred feet. Its restless noise beckoned Kinthup day and night. He had been able to save a spare compass that the lama didn't know about; he'd take it out after the day's work, when everyone had turned in. The needle would pulsate with the murmur of the stream and continue to buzz in his head like an insect. One day, he went to fetch firewood in the forest and didn't return. It was a day in March, more than six months after he'd been sold to the dzongpon.

But even as he took to his heels, Kinthup never strayed

far from the Tsangpo. He cut his path through dark forests and cliffs. Following the compass's needle, keeping count of his footsteps on prayer beads, Kinthup pushed on for days, committing every bend and sandbar, every rapid and feeder into memory. Sometimes he spent the night in a deserted yak-grazers' shed, but more often in caves and on treetops, surviving on wild mushrooms and leaves. After five days, he came to a spot where the Tsangpo leapt across a sharp fall, forming a cloud of spray, with a rainbow shimmering on it. At another spot he found fresh human footprints on the desolate riverbank. On the eleventh day Kinthup entered an enchanting green valley ringed with snow-clad mountains. This was Pemako. The river meandered across the narrow fertile valley and, on the brow of a hill, was a monastery. This was Marpung.

Men from Tongkyuk were waiting there, they caught Kinthup as he entered the monastery. But the kind abbot gave them 50 rupees and released Kinthup, on the condition that he would serve there to pay for his freedom.

After the slavery in Tongkyuk, life in Marpung was easy. Thirty monks lived in the gompa. Kinthup darned their robes, worked in the kitchen and fetched provisions from the village below once every two days. From this enchanting valley the Tsangpo rushed into the impenetrable gorge after a series of rapids. On clear days, the river could be seen from the monastery's terrace, gleaming like a strip of molten silver. The calls of golden eagles were borne upon the breeze. At day's end, his work done, Kinthup would sit at the temple door and pray, his gaze fixed on the huge painted eyes of Buddha lit up by a butter lamp. Counting beads on his finger day after day, to measure distances, the passage of time, to mumble 'Om mani padme hum' before the Lord, to rejig his memories of landscape and topography—the rosary itself seemed to have become a river. He'd wake up at night and see the glaciers shining like pyramids of crystal against a star-spangled sky. The murmur of the Tsangpo would rise from the mist-wrapped valley like a person talking in sleep. One day Kinthup went to the Khenpo, the venerable abbot, and prayed for leave to go on a pilgrimage. By this time, he had spent four months in Marpung; it had been two years since he had set out from Darjeeling. The Khenpo granted his prayer.

Kinthup followed the river's downward course, resuming his interrupted mission, toiling around giant boulders and across precipitous cliffs. Sometimes he followed the tracks that herds of wild takin, a species of antelope, used on their winter migration. The more he pushed on, the more the path grew forbidding, sheer walls covered with stunted alpine bushes reached up to the skies, networks of thick lianas hanging from ancient trees cast the darkness of night in daytime. Not the call of a beast, not the warble of a bird, only the ear-splitting roar of the Tsangpo rushing down the narrowest of defiles. After eight days, Kinthup reached a bend where there was a strip of yellow sandy bank and, 200 feet above it, a cave. For five days, he worked from sunrise to sunset to carve five hundred foot-long sticks out of rhododendron wood. He stored them inside the cave and returned to Marpung.

Two months later, after winter had given way to summer and the snow had melted over the passes, Kinthup prayed again for another pilgrimage—the great Tsari pilgrimage that took place every twelve years. This time, too, he was allowed to go. But Kinthup went to Lhasa instead and got in touch with a Kazi, a minor official from Sikkim. He talked the Kazi into writing a letter to Nem Singh in Darjeeling. The letter, addressed to Harman Sahib, narrated his plight and how he planned to throw five hundred specially marked wooden sticks into the river Tsangpo nine months later on a specified date. This was according to a plan Harman had himself devised. Men were to be stationed at points where the Brahmaputra entered the plains of Assam, and the finding of a single marked stick would prove conclusively that Tsangpo *was* Brahmaputra.

From Lhasa, Kinthup came back to Marpung monastery, to a life of clockwork labour, to the hypnotic eyes of the Buddha lighted by a yak-butter lamp, to the call of eagles and the riparian whispers rising up at night from the sleeping valley. Days passed, the moon waxed and waned, the rains returned to Pemakȯ and turned it a resplendent green. Kinthup petitioned again, for another pilgrimage.

This time the Khenpo, addressed as Khen Rinpoche, granted him freedom. He also gave the Indian a leg of sun-dried mutton, cheese and a few Tibetan coins for the road. Kinthup offered a prayer in the temple, took leave of the monks, and set out for that cave in the gorge.

But the Tsangpo was swollen with rains, the tracks along its banks had vanished. It took him fifteen days to cover a distance that he'd trekked earlier in eight days. On reaching the spot before the assigned day, Kinthup found the narrow bank flooded and water almost reaching the lip of the cave. He tied the metal tags that Harman Sahib had given him in Darjeeling—which he'd been carrying all these years tied to his waist like amulets—to each of the sticks. Then he tossed them into the stream in batches of fifty for the next ten days.

Seven miles downstream from this spot, the Tsangpo cut its way through a gully, rounded a bend to the south and entered the constriction between the Namche Barwa and Gyala Peri, both seven-thousanders. For the next 50 miles, it ran along an unbelievably deep and narrow course, the heart of the Tsangpo gorge, into which sunlight scarcely entered in the daytime. There was no path or ledge across the near vertical cliffs that rose to dizzying heights. It would take one hundred and twenty years for man to cover these 50 miles. Long after both the poles, all the deserts, continents and much of the ocean floors had been explored, long after men had set foot on the moon, a team of European adventurers would kayak down this stretch. In 2002. By that time, however, satellite cameras had accurately mapped the river's fascinating course.

A hundred and twenty years is a long time. Many adventurers would come in the meantime in search of a great waterfall with a shimmering rainbow, as Kinthup had described it. But on that occasion he himself was not carrying the burden of consequent history. After dispatching the sticks, he skirted the 50-mile gorge and followed the Tsangpo downstream as far as he could. His plan was to enter India through the gap in the mountains cut by the river. For days, he trekked up and down sharp hills clothed in some of the densest and moist evergreen forests in the Himalaya, where it rained for most of the year and strange life forms thrived; sought shelter in the dwellings of mysterious tribesmen on hilltops reached by rope ladders; ate snakes and geckos; and almost reached the Indian frontier. From a village named Onlet, gazing southwards, Kinthup had a dream-like vision: the wave upon wave of mountains ceased abruptly before the endless alluvial plains of a delta and, over this delta, the great river meandered, like a braid of mist stretched to the horizon.

But his plan to come back to India was thwarted by the Abor tribesmen who inhabited the region, whose hostility to outsiders was as old as the mountains. Kinthup had to retrace his steps and he returned to Darjeeling via Tsetang, a city to the southeast of Lhasa. It was the 17th of November, 1884.

Four years had elapsed since he'd set out. Darjeeling had changed beyond recognition. A narrow-gauge mountain railway had been laid, the bazaar at the end of Cart Road had grown in size, people of all castes and calling had settled around it. Kinthup returned to an alien, heartless town to learn that his wife and baby daughter had died. Nem Singh, too, had passed away; the letter he'd sent Singh had been kept unopened. On top of it all, Lieutenant Henry Harman had gone back to England on sick leave and had died there. No one had waited in the plains of Assam to receive the sticks Kinthup had floated in the river. Not a soul in Darjeeling was willing to listen to, let alone believe in, the story of an illiterate tailor.

Daylight had faded when I stepped out of the bookshop on Mall Road. The lights of Chhota Shimla glowed on the distant hill. The Ridge overflowed with the evening crowd. Screeching children in gay woollens ran about, groups of young people thronged the chaat parlours. The locals, too, had turned out on evening walks with their dogs; a coquettish poodle was courting a grave Rottweiler at Scandal Point. Perky mannequins ranged before the shops, their fibre skin and nylon hair aglitter. Suddenly it began to drizzle. The wet asphalt shone like a mirror with the reflection of people running helter-skelter for cover. I slipped into the grey air of the Indian Coffee House.

Jawaharlal Nehru is said to have supped here. The ancient wooden menu board above the till said that it still served British-style noodles, not the American chowmien. The sullen waiters in stained liveries, the paint-peeled furniture and the chipped crockery brought back to me memories of another iconic coffee house, in Kolkata's College Street, on a winter's evening. But this one exuded a staid charm. Besides, where else on Shimla's Mall Road could one sit for hours with an 8-rupee cup of infusion and let the eyes roam across the window to study leggy belles prancing on the street? A bunch of lawyers chatted at a corner table, their black coats hanging from the backs of their chairs like detachable wings. A lone old man in a grey serge jacket and homburg slowly turned a spoon in his cup and looked up expectantly at the entrance from time to time.

The story of Kinthup befogged my head. I felt like the marriage guest in Coleridge's 'Rime of the Ancient Mariner'. The ancient mariner, of long grey beard and glittering eyes, clasps the marriage guest's wrist and snaps: 'There was a ship!' Then he unburdens his tale. And here a dowdy old tailor had emerged from the pages of yellowing documents and had gripped my mind with the words: 'There was a river!' From Nima Tashi's shop in Darjeeling to the antique bookshop in Shimla, he'd been chasing me around with his story.

After Kinthup returned to Darjeeling, nobody was willing to attach much value to the account of his adventure. He had no documentary evidence with him, neither a note nor the sketch of a map to support his claim. It took the Survey of India two years to put together a brief narrative report of Kinthup's route. It was transcribed by a lama and then translated into English by a native clerk. As the oral testimony passed through two languages, the details became muddled and inconsistencies crept in. The report was consigned to the damp recesses of the mahafezkhana to attract mould and wait for the arsonists of a statehood agitation in another century. Kinthup in the meantime returned to his old calling, to a tailoring shop in the bazaar, to darn a life tattered by four years of exile.

Time had not only turned a full circle for him, it had leapt forward to another level altogether. In 1903, a military expedition was sent to Tibet. In one fell swoop, the whole enterprise of espionage became redundant. In the hands of professional geographers, the last undiscovered corner of the earth finally appeared on maps in vivid outlines, with its mountains, forests and valleys. A single detail that continued to remain an enigma was the shape of a line, the path of a river.

A native tailor's mission to the Tsangpo failed to receive the attention it deserved, but his name sometimes appeared in the writings of explorers. That was because Kinthup had mentioned a waterfall that he'd seen on the Tsangpo. A river that rushed down from a plateau 12,000 feet high to almost sea level in just 200 miles cried out for a grand waterfall, grander than the Niagara or the Victoria, or even a series of falls. The one that Kinthup had mentioned, on whose misty spray hung a permanent rainbow, fired the imagination of explorers.

One of them was Eric Bailey—also known as Frederick Marshman Bailey—an officer who had been part of the military campaign to Tibet in 1903. That was when he first became curious about this great river. Ten years later, together with Henry Morshead, an officer in the Survey of India, he attempted to approach the great Tsangpo gorge upriver from the Dihang Valley. They failed to enter it but were deeply impressed by Kinthup's incredible mission thirty years earlier.

By then the geopolitics of Southeast Asia had changed. The fall of the Qing dynasty in 1912 had loosened China's grip on Tibet. The British saw this as a window of opportunity and called a meeting at Shimla in March 1913 to draw a clear-cut border line between India and Tibet. It was supposed to be a tri-partite agreement between the governments of India, Tibet and China but the Chinese withdrew before the signing of the agreement.

That was when a search for an old man began in Darjeeling. He was eventually found in a hole-in-the-wall tailoring shop in Chowkbazaar and taken to Shimla. It was springtime in the summer capital: carnations and petunias bloomed in the gardens and on waysides, and the crest of Jakku Hill was still touched with snow. But the old man could not enjoy the beauty. Long hours of needlework in poorly lit shops had dimmed his eyesight. His body, too, had grown decrepit. And yet, for four days, he mined the veins of memory and reeled out before the officers of the Tibet Frontier Commission an astonishingly vivid description of the last unexplored region on earth.

This time Captain Eric Bailey himself acted as his interpreter. Bailey had spent enough time in the eastern Himalaya to learn the languages spoken there. Armed with this testimony and the survey data gathered by Bailey and Morshead, the Foreign Secretary, Henry McMahon, drew a red line on a small-scale map (where 1 inch equalled 8 miles) with a felt nib. An imaginary boundary running over high knotted ridges, watersheds, mountain passes and valleys, it would later be known as the McMahon Line and engender a lot of disquiet and bloodshed.

The old man was awarded a medal and 1,000 rupees as a token of recognition for his service. Captain Bailey had lobbied to get him a pension, but it was turned down; the government was of the opinion that this man with his incredible memory would live long and be a drain on the exchequer.

The old man returned to Darjeeling and died a few months later. He, Kinthup, had been living only to tell his tale.

It was late in the evening when I emerged from the coffee house. Most of the shops had closed, the Mall Road was empty and dark. Three shadowy porters with huge loads on their backs were trudging towards Lakkar Bazaar. The lights of Chhota Shimla had dimmed on the distant hillside. The path to Summer Hill was eerily animated with the chorus of crickets and the quivering chiaroscuro cast by streetlamps over the gently swaying branches of trees. Not a soul could be seen there. A 2-kilometre trek down this path seemed to me a daunting task; the shuttle bus was an easier option.

The shops in the Middle Bazaar, too, had closed. The winding alleyways were haunted by listless porters, drunkards and street dogs. At the tailors' mohulla, the hum of a lonely sewing machine rose and fell, mimicking a cricket's call. Did Kinthup stay here during his time in Shimla? A century ago, this part of the town must have been bigger and more crowded. Readymade garments were yet to arrive and the tailor community worked from here for the Mall Road clothiers. The flurry of parties, races and fancy-dress balls must have ensured that the sewing machines here never stopped.

Below this mohulla was the yeasty upheave of Lower Bazaar's packed tin roofs, which Rudyard Kipling compares to a crowded rabbit warren in his novel *Kim*. 'A man who knows his way here can defy all the police of India's summer capital'—the writer had claimed—'so cunningly does a veranda communicate with a veranda, alley-way with alley-way, and bolt-hole with bolt-hole.'

Nothing seemed to have changed. Narrow, dimly lit lanes squeezed through dingy squatter settlements where families were cooking dinner upon braziers right at their doorsteps. Upon a missing window pane covered over with old newspapers, the silhouette of a girl's head swung like a clockwork doll as she read aloud from a primer. Her companions were playing hopscotch on the alley steps. A group of women beat washings with wooden clubs around a community tap. I picked a shortcut through Ladakhi Mohulla, around what had once been the haunt of jhampanis, the rickshaw-pullers of yore, and climbed down a steep flight of stairs directly to the bus terminus. Boxes of apples were being loaded on to the roofs of overnight buses heading to Chandigarh and other distant cities. The conductor of the last town bus to Summer Hill was calling:

'Boileau Ganj! Tutu! Jutogh! … Last trip!'

Memories of another hill town sprang to mind. Many years ago, as evening would fall in Darjeeling's Chowkbazaar, the drivers of local service jeeps would call out:

'Silgarhi! Kharsang! Silgarhi! … Last turn!'

Each time I heard that call, I'd feel a stab of homesickness. I had to fight the urge to get into a jeep and escape to the plains. Now, after all these years, the memories brought back to me a strange yearning for Darjeeling.

The Shangri-La Bar

In Darjeeling's Chowkbazaar, a flight of stairs behind the Golghar Restaurant led to a row of tailoring shops. These shops had been there since the early days of the town. The lane always buzzed with a flurry of sewing machines running non-stop, though nothing could be heard from the street below due to the din of peddlers and traffic. But on wet monsoon afternoons, when a brief lull would set in the bazaar, or late into the night before a big festival like Diwali or Eid, one could hear the machines from a distance. Sometimes they sounded like the murmur of a secret spring, at others, a chorus of cicadas. The clientele of these tailoring shops came from the town's poor working classes. Cheap jackets and salwar suits were made here round the year, torn garments were darned. But during the festivals colourful dawra-sural, chowbandi-faria and other gay ethnic wear glittered in the dim shops.

After I stumbled into Kinthup's story at Nima Tashi's shop, this part of the town began to interest me. Every other day I'd make a detour through here, for no particular reason, on my way to Chowrasta and back. Master tailors sat behind rusty Singer machines with measuring tapes coiled around their necks and stubs of pencils tucked behind ears. Their old, doddering assistants sat on the floors, hunched over piles of frayed garments.

Did anyone here know a man named Kinthup?

In Satyajit Ray's *Kanchenjungha*, shot entirely on location in Darjeeling, a small local boy had a cameo role. Nothing was known about him except that the film's title card had a name, the only Nepali name, in the list of actors: Gnuiye. The film was made in 1962. Thirty years later, armed with a snapshot of the boy in the film, I had made a frantic search for Gnuiye around town. I wanted to write a feature on him for a magazine. And I'd found him one day in a squatters' colony in Tungsung: he was exactly that same boy in appearance and age, unchanged despite the intervening years. What if a search for Kinthup brought forth that same old man? What if he emerged from the dim depth of a shop, drawing away the cobwebs of a century, and turned his bleary eyes at me from behind thick glasses?

I didn't take the risk, but neither did the thought cease to haunt me.

From the tailors' lane, up along the winding path to Chowrasta, was Nima Tashi's kabari shop. A bunch of pimply schoolboys would gather there in the afternoon and root through old copies of *Debonair* and *Playboy* for crumbs of masturbatory fantasy. I'd browse the paperbacks swept out of hotel rooms, most of which were dog-eared, torn and printed in different European languages. One day I found a copy of James Hilton's *Lost Horizon*.

Published in 1933, under the gathering shadows of the Second World War, *Lost Horizon* had been a cult novel. It was here that a valley named Shangri-La had first made its appearance. The story begins with a plane carrying six kidnapped Europeans from Afghanistan crash-landing on a snowbound wilderness somewhere in Tibet. A lama rescues them and takes them to a monastery in Shangri-La. Hidden in the depth of a gorge bound on all sides by snow-clad mountains, this is a valley of eternal spring where life flows in a delightfully slow rhythm. A river meanders across the green narrow valley and the monastery sits on a cliff. A secret haven, cut off from the outside world, and yet provided with all the amenities of modern civilization; a place whose inhabitants even have longer lifespans than their contemporaries elsewhere.

This utopia had cast a spell upon a generation of Western men and women shaken by the horrors of war and the fast pace of urban life. Shangri-La became a symbol of the mysterious Orient; a fictitious valley became a global brand name for pubs, hotels, spas, perfumes, whisky and aphrodisiacs.

From Nima Tashi's shop, I would tramp up Nehru Road to the traffic chowki where three roads met, take the right flank at Keventer's and climb up, pass by Das Studio, Glenary's and stop before a trim white European cottage with peaked green roofs. This, too, was Shangri-La—a hotel and bar-cum-restaurant. During noontime, a notice would hang on its doorknob: 'Happy Hour—up to 4 p.m.' I would push open the door and enter a wide hall with polished parquet flooring, tall bay windows and a few not-so-happy souls at small square tables. The air would be suffused with the scent of warm walnut, Worcestershire sauce and Eric Clapton being played at a low volume. A couple of waiters would stand at the bar counter, dozing with their chins propped on folded arms. I would settle in a window-side seat, gulp down a large peg of Old Monk rum in the nick of Happy Hour and look outside. A grey fog would fan out slowly over the rust-brown tin roofs of the town below. At the next table a Scandinavian tourist couple would sip Diet Coke and talk in quick bird-like voices with a fat guidebook open before them.

At a corner table, a middle-aged executive would sit motionless, his face completely blank, his tie loosened, the foam on his mug of beer long dead.

My days in Darjeeling followed one another like flocks of suicidal sheep over a cliff of amnesia. I felt inside me the claws of depression that many men had felt here before me, especially during the endless months of rain. By then the excitement of coming to work in a famous hill town had worn off. Like a wisp of mist I drifted from moment to moment, from the Mall to Chowkbazaar, from the rounds of card games at the teachers' hostel to late-night films on Star Movies, from the story of a 19th-century tailor-spy to Happy Hour at Shangri-La Bar.

Did the idea of Shangri-La come from the valley where Kinthup had fled to escape slavery? There, too, a river meandered through a narrow valley hidden between the mountains, and there was a monastery on a hill. He had spent many months there.

On a wall of the Shangri-La bar hung a framed picture of a curious Last Supper. It was an imitation of Da Vinci's famous painting, but instead of Jesus and his twelve disciples, there were the Buddha and an equal number of sramanas sitting at a table laden with food and drinks.

Did Buddha, too, have a last supper with his followers? I called on Professor Lopsang Norbu to find out.

Norbu taught Tibetan language and literature at Government College and stayed in the teachers' quarters across the campus. Every day, after lunch hour, he could be seen entering the college premises, impeccably dressed in a three-piece suit, a felt hat and with a large umbrella; the umbrella would either be held open over his head or neatly folded and carried as a walking stick.

He rarely spoke to anyone and never attended faculty meetings. There'd always be an expression of deep calm on his face, and a slowness in his movements that had nothing to do with age—Norbu was in his early fifties and looked quite fit. It was rumoured that he hailed from a wealthy family in Tibet that had brought yak-loads of gold when they fled into India with the Dalai Lama. Another story claimed that Norbu had spent his childhood in the Tibetan Refugee Center in Nayabasti. None of these claims were verifiable, but one would always find him at the head of the annual procession during Lhosar, the Tibetan New Year, dressed in the flowing ceremonial robe.

The Tibetan department was on the second floor of the main building, at the end of a narrow corridor that also led to my department. We would nod and smile at each other whenever we passed and, on a bright sunny day, he'd respond to my 'good morning' with, 'Yes, a very good morning indeed!' and flash a gold-capped tooth. He invited me to his cubicle when I met him in the corridor with my query.

'Yes, like Jesus, Buddha had partaken of food before his death. But it was not exactly like the event of the Last Supper. The Lord had turned eighty, his body had grown frail after the hardship of long peregrinations. He had decided to leave the corporal body and take parinirvana. On that hallowed day, at a place near Kushinagar, Buddha took his last meal from Chandu the ironsmith. It was a dish named sukaramaddava. There is a debate among scholars about what exactly sukaramaddava was. Was it the meat of a wild boar or a type of mushroom? Well, we must keep in mind that Buddha was not a strict vegetarian. Anyway, unlike Jesus, our Lord didn't share the food with his followers. Rather he did the opposite: he directed Chandu to bury the leftovers immediately. After this he came to a saal grove near the river. That was when he felt pain in the stomach. The Lord achieved nirvana soon enough. But it was not death by food poisoning.'

Next day, I took to Norbu the report of Kinthup's mission that I had found in Nima Tashi's shop. When I pulled the crumbling, mould-spotted thing out of a polythene bag, he was taken aback; but he recovered quickly, put on his reading glasses and took a long careful look.

Norbu had never heard Kinthup's name, nor had he read anywhere about this clandestine mission into Tibet. But he knew about Ugyen Gyatso, the man who had transcribed Kinthup's oral testimony before it was translated into English. Ugyen Gyatso had been a well-known Tibetologist, he told me.

'He was a lama from the Rinchenpong monastery in Sikkim,' Norbu said. 'Soon after they founded Darjeeling, the British government set up the Bhutia Boarding School. Gyatso was appointed a teacher there. Sarat Chandra Das, the Bengali from Calcutta, was the headmaster. Surely you know about Sarat Babu?'

I shook my head.

Norbu gave a sad smile, pulled out a big fat book from a shelf and placed it on the table before me. It was *The Tibetan English Dictionary–with Sanskrit Synonyms*, by Sarat Chandra Das. A black cloth-bound volume with more than a thousand pages, it sat like an altar on the table.

'He was a true pioneer. This book was first published in 1902. Nobody has yet been able to surpass this work. Perhaps you Bengalis didn't give him the recognition that was his due, but it's impossible to study Tibetan language and culture without acknowledging Sarat Babu's contribution.'

Norbu put his reading glasses back into the case and continued distractedly:

'I've never heard about Kinthup, but it is a fact that the British government used to send spies into Tibet in the 19th century. Some of them were from Darjeeling. They had set up this school to teach the hill people science and the English language. Sarat Chandra Das was appointed for this purpose. But that was not his only identity.'

Norbu didn't say anything more on that day. I, too, didn't prod him. A few days later on an afternoon, browsing at the Oxford Bookstore on Chowrasta, I found a book: *Journey to Central Tibet and Lhasa* by Sarat Chandra Das. The book was based on the journal Das had kept during his secret expedition to Tibet in 1881–82. As I flipped through the pages, I found Ugyen Gyatso's name a number of times. I bought the book and went directly to Professor Norbu's residence.

It was one of those old tin-roofed wooden bungalows that would soon be torn down to make way for concrete structures. Evening was falling when I rang the doorbell. Norbu himself opened the door; he was wearing a blue corduroy dressing gown. A look of surprise lit up his face as he welcomed me into the drawing-room. In spite of the warped wall panels, stains of seepage on the ceiling, and other signs of disrepair, the room was tastefully done up. Woollen rugs draped the floor and sofa sets, brightly painted silk pelmets hung from the door frames, a beautiful jade Buddha sat in a bookshelf and large posters of Dalai Lama and Free Tibet were adorned with khadas, ceremonial silk scarves. Cinders glowed in a copper brazier inside the fireplace.

I handed Norbu the book I'd just bought. He took a quick

look at it and gave me an amused smile; his gold-capped tooth caught the gleam of the cinders.

'It's been a long time since I have found a Bengali from Calcutta showing interest in Sarat Babu,' he said affectionately.

I learnt that the book was based on Sarat Das's second journey into Tibet; the first one had happened a year earlier. Ugyen Gyatso was his companion on both the occasions. Sarat Chandra went as a British spy, assuming the fake identity of a Buddhist scholar, and had won the trust of the Panchen Lama's prime minister.

Norbu showed me a very old edition of the same book bound in green leather, published by the Royal Geographic Society of England. It had a number of photographs and half-tone sketches which were not in the paperback I'd bought. At the back of the title page was a sketch of a young man swaddled in Tibetan clothes, riding a yak across a mountain pass.

'Read the book,' Norbu said. 'This is the record of a fascinating journey. Das went there as a spy, on a secret mission. But that was far surpassed by a deep and respectful curiosity about my country: its nature, climate, people and culture.'

I turned the pages of the old book to see the photographs: a Lepcha soldier with thin braided hair and a peacock feather on his hat; a procession of mourners in peaked caps and stringed musical instruments in their hands walking in the wake of a hearse; a frail princess weighed down with jewellery staring nervously at the camera; a cane bridge spanning a deep gorge cut by a foaming torrent; a tea-drinking ceremony of the elites under a painted marquee in a forest clearing; a ritual dance of lamas sporting bizarre masks; the majestic Potala Palace at Lhasa; a frozen waterfall...

A thin young girl dressed in a chuba entered the room on cat-like feet, carrying tea in covered porcelain cups. A small dog with black and white fur followed her in. It leapt upon Norbu's lap and began to inspect the stranger, showing a scarlet tongue.

Norbu introduced her to me as his daughter. She was studying for an M.A. degree in Jawaharlal Nehru University in Delhi and had come home on vacation.

'Were these photographs taken during that mission?' I asked.

The girl twisted her neck daintily to look at the book open on my lap, but left the room before Norbu replied.

'Sarat Babu himself had taken them,' he said. 'He was carrying a glass plate camera and loads of photographic equipment. There was also a telescope, a magic lantern, books on science, and smallpox vaccines. A large number of people died of this cursed disease every year in Tibet. And yes, he was also carrying a complete lithographic press.'

'Was the British government trying to send a message through these equipment of modern science?' I asked.

Norbu laughed out loud and shook his head. The dog pricked up its tail and turned to look at his face.

'From the point of view of Western science, Tibet still was in the middle ages. But the British never had any such lofty purpose. Their sole objective was to gain knowledge of the country's topography and system of commerce. The equipment were being procured from Calcutta by Sengchen Dorjechen, the Panchen Lama's prime minister, through Sarat Chandra Das. Sengchen was a very important and respected lama. Sarat Chandra became his great friend during his first visit. The friendship was based on mutual admiration. Sarat took lessons in theology from the great priest and, in return, taught him English, arithmetic and the technology of the camera, the telegraph and other instruments. In fact, Sengchen was so deeply impressed by Western science that he'd begun to write a book on photography in Tibetan. He was a rare genius, his friendship with this English-educated young man from Bengal, too, was very strange. It had a tragic end, though. But I'm not going to tell that to you now. That'll spoil the pleasure of reading this book.'

Norbu fell silent and began to run his fingers through the woolly neck of the dog. A pensive expression came upon his face. A light rain drummed on the bungalow's tin roof.

'Everything is written on the wheel of fortune,' he said softly. 'If that writing had been different, if Western science could disseminate into Tibet through the efforts of venerable Sengchen, the history of this subcontinent would have been completely different.'

He seemed to have grown distant as he intoned these words; he came back presently and smiled.

'But let it be. Perhaps you and I wouldn't be sitting here together if that had happened. In any case, the older generation of Tibetans living in Darjeeling still have a place for Sarat Babu in their hearts. And for good reason too. He did the most significant work of his life from a village near this town, from his bungalow named Lhasa Villa.'

In 1874 Darjeeling was only a cluster of log cabins and a bazaar on top of a wooded mountain at the end of a long rough trail from the plains. Its fame as a summer resort was still a few years away. That year, in the month of April, a twenty-five-year-old man set out on foot from the town of Siliguri at dawn and reached Kalabari in the afternoon. Shaded by ancient saal and fig trees, Kalabari was the last little village in the Terai. There was a dak bungalow here, perched at a height of about 200 feet. The young man sent the bungalow's caretaker into the village before nightfall and, after some haggling, hired a pony and a pair of coolies from the local Mech tribe. Next morning he set off on the uphill journey to Darjeeling. It was a two-day march, with night halts in dak bungalows at places called Kurseong and Sonada. The young man had never ridden a pony before.

Never before had he set his eyes on a mountain either. Born in a village in the flat plains of East Bengal, he was preparing for a civil engineering degree from Calcutta's Presidency College. He was a sharp and diligent student, and had drawn the attention of his sahib teachers early. The dreaded tropical malaria stalked Calcutta in those days. It had struck our young man and had debilitated him. It was one of his teachers, a botanist and the inspector of schools, who first advised the young man to go to Darjeeling and take up the headmaster's job in a newly opened boarding school for local Bhutia boys.

'Go to Darjeeling,' Professor C.B. Clarke had said. 'Arthur Campbell has set up a nice little sanatorium at 7,000 feet. It has fine home weather and a most picturesque scenery. I believe you'll recover your health there. You have a promising future, young man, and I'm sure that future is awaiting you in Darjeeling.'

Everything seemed to be going according to a plan. Just when the young Bengali from Calcutta was marching to Darjeeling, Sir Alfred Croft, the Director of Public Instruction, was writing a confidential letter to A.C. Lyall, the Foreign Secretary of India.

For quite some time, the British government in India had been sending spies into Tibet. They were recruited from the hill tribes of north India, given basic training in topographic survey, and were sent disguised as itinerant monks or merchants. Their physical features made it easier for them to get through the heavily guarded mountain passes. Moreover, they could survive the hardship of travelling in high, rugged terrain. But there was a catch: none of these men had any formal education, and they lacked the scientific attitude that was needed to collect the in-depth knowledge of the unknown land, its people and cultures, which the British hungered for. A new generation of English-educated Indians were required for this job. Such a young man was being sent to Darjeeling.

This was the gist of Croft's letter to the Foreign Secretary. But the young man didn't have an inkling of it. His mind was filled with a vague excitement as he was about to begin a new chapter in his life far away from the plains of Bengal. He was already married, his wife stayed in their village home. During the long journey from there to Siliguri by train, boat, mail coach and ox cart, he was visited by memories of her, of a nose stud and a tear gleaming on a diffident face under the diaphanous shadow of a mustard-yellow sari. But those memories faded soon after he mounted the pony, a newly broken nut-brown mare, and began to notice the breathtaking scenery around him. As the narrow bridle path corkscrewed up the hill, range upon range of verdant mountains unfurled before his eyes. A dark primeval forest closed in from all sides, with giant, centuries-old trees, from whose branches thick creepers hung like ropes from the masts of ships he had seen at Calcutta's shipyard. After about 2,000 feet, the view of the smoke-hazed plains receded away behind clumps of bamboo and tree ferns. He left the tropical forest of plantain and fig, alive with birdsong, and entered a land of giant oaks, birches and mists, where a prehistoric silence was scarcely ruffled by the murmur of a spring. Sometimes the mountains echoed with the call of an unknown beast. En route he passed groups of coolies: they were trekking uphill in slow motion with huge loads tied to their backs, their feet shod in strips of leather caked with blood. On reaching Kurseong, he saw the Kanchenjunga for the first time: it appeared like a wave of pure crystal miraculously floating in the sky. He heard the church bells of Hope Town, passed a Lepcha village named Ghum, turned a bend and saw in the distance a clutch of white cottages upon a narrow spur. This was Darjeeling.

John Edgar, ICS, was the Deputy Commissioner there. On reaching the town, the young man went to the commissioner's office and introduced himself as Babu Sarat Chandra Das. An accommodation was arranged for him at Alice Villa, a boarding house on Mount Pleasant Road. Next day he joined service.

A BROCKEN SPECTRE

'As none of the Company's servants, and I might almost say no European, had ever visited the country which I was about to enter, I was equally in the dark as to the road, the climate, or the people.'

—George Bogle, *Narratives*

'At a subsequent interview he [Mr. John Edgar, ICS] gave me three more books including Markham's Mission of George Bogle and Thomas Manning to Tibet in 1776 and 1841. I read the last book over and over again. It kindled in my mind a burning desire for visiting Tibet and for exploring its unknown tracts.'

—Sarat Chandra Das, *Autobiography*

Lhasa Villa

Rare is the man who has ever come to stay in Darjeeling from the plains and has never once been bitten by depression. In the mid-19th century, a sanatorium was set up for invalid British soldiers at Senchal, a wooded hill on the outskirts of the town, but it had to be abandoned soon because of a string of suicides. This continued even after Darjeeling became a popular hill station. A lone executive sitting at a pub with a mug of beer, or a listless college teacher clinging on to Happy Hour knew it. It was a type of dark solitude that flowed about the town like a network of subterranean springs.

With so many hill stations in India, was this unique to Darjeeling? Was it because of the tenacious fog, the dampness, and the absence of the sun for long months? Or did it stem from Darjeeling's unique topography? From the plains of the Terai, after crossing a series of connected ridges, one reached this town perched on the edge of a narrow spur that shot into a deep valley, ringed on three sides by a stadium of high mountain ranges. To the tourist it was a most picturesque scene, but to the exile it could be the edge of an abyss. It would usually take two to three monsoons to come to terms with those dark feelings. Many would return to the plains before that, quitting a job or on a transfer of workplace, taking back the memories of a grey light oozing through fog, a light that cast no shadow, and the rank smell of moss.

A century after Sarat Chandra Das came to this town, I was bitten by this dark feeling. In those days I was staying in a rented apartment on Convent Road; from the window of my bedroom I could see the Happy Valley tea garden below and a part of the district prison. The euphoria of being on my own in a famous hill town had evaporated by then. It was my second rainy season in Darjeeling. The world would remain shrouded in fog throughout the day, making the approach of night stealthy and imperceptible. Sleep wouldn't come to the cold bed strewn with old paperbacks and magazines from Nima Tashi's shop. A sharp lonely face on the Penguin Classics cover of Camus' *The Outsider* (a painting by Jacques Villon) would turn its empty eye sockets at the sun-glazed *Playboy* girl, with a young, balding Pablo Neruda watching this languid courtship from the cover of *Residence on Earth*. The lines from the book of poems, written during the young poet's lonely days in Ceylon, would swim inside my head; they would belch bubbles, peck at the moss of sad lust growing in the folds of my brain.

One of my bedroom walls was actually the side of a hill. During the rainy months, beads of water would appear and trickle down like sweat. But running water was scarce. I would hear at midnight a strange wind rasp and moan through the bone-dry bathroom pipes. I returned late on an evening to find that water from the municipal supply line had flowed through a faucet, left inadvertently open, and had flooded the floors. Cigarette stubs, slippers, and the newspaper that had come in the afternoon mail were floating on it. I waded in through ankle-deep water, spread the soggy newspaper under the table lamp and flopped down on the bed after swallowing four Diazepam tablets. As I began to sink into a glutinous sleep, I saw vapours rising from the newspaper in the shaft of lamp light, and a line of letters coiling up like tiny black insects. Green buds were peeping out of the hillside wall, uncurling, shooting tendrils across the room, creepers slithered over the floor and choked the door. I wiped my hand across my face and it felt strangely unfamiliar; the portrait on *The Outsider*'s cover was clasped on it like a mask.

When I woke up, I couldn't make out if it was morning or afternoon. My head felt hollow inside. Had I died in sleep? I opened the door and stepped out into the balcony. Electric lights were coming on below in the market, but daylight still lingered high up over the hill top. I put on a jacket over my pyjamas and began to drift down the winding path like a feather. Down a few hundred feet, the cobbled path gave way to a dirt track into the tea garden, across straggling tea bushes that hadn't been pruned for years. It led along the spine of a spur to a sharp khud. An old chorten, crumbling and smothered by the thick roots of a tree, stood there. Once upon a time, before the tea garden had come up, this must have been a sacred place. Dogs were barking in the distance, evening dusk had fallen in the workers' quarters below, the cloud above the Observatory Hill had lifted to let in the rays of the setting sun. As I stood there motionlessly, a wind began and churned up the fog over the khud. The barking of the dogs ceased and an eerie silence fell. Suddenly a tunnel of light formed in the whorl of fog, a ring-shaped rainbow appeared on it. In its deep centre was the shadow of a man, as in a hologram, its head turned towards me.

I learnt later that this miracle is known as the Brocken Spectre; it was my own shadow. On very rare occasions, particularly on the edge of a cliff, such shadows are cast by the sun's rays refracted in the fog. The magic of the Spectre depends on the density of the water particles in the fog and the position of the viewer relative to the angle of the sun. The shadow is so named because the phenomenon is frequently seen from a hilltop in Germany named Brocken.

I have never believed in the supernatural. But on that day, as I watched the giant shadow staring back at me from the void above the ravine, I felt a mystic sensation pass through me. Its impact lingered long and didn't lessen even after I learnt the science behind it.

It was on a moonlit night in November that Sarat Chandra Das set off from Darjeeling on his secret mission to Tibet. His anxious eyes were scanning the distant mountains of east Nepal for signs of fresh snow. Caught between the fear of death and an irrepressible urge to conquer all obstacles, he left the sleeping town on a pony. This was his second foray into the forbidden land in less than two years. This time the government had raised his salary from 40 rupees per month to three hundred. He wasn't permitted to share any detail of the mission with anyone, not even his wife. He had written to her that he would be away in Shigatse for a few days on official work. Naturally, the simple village woman didn't know where Shigatse was, or the nature of her husband's work, or the fact that the government had made provision for her a widow's pension if he never returned.

No one except a pair of Bhutia men saw Sarat leaving the town at such a late hour on a chill winter's night. The sounds of drums, pipes and rustic songs were coming from a distant settlement of coolies, ruffling the silence. He met Ugyen Gyatso on the bank of the Rangeet. The river was full and hushed. The party of seven men—comprising Sarat, Ugyen, their servant Phurchung, the cook and porters—crossed it over bamboos laid across. At half past one in the morning they reached a derelict place named Gok.

On an earlier visit to Sikkim two years ago, Sarat had seen a dozen shops at Gok. Upcountry traders used to come here to buy cardamom and maize and take them to the market in Darjeeling. But now only a cowshed stood there, where a Nepali man was snoring away. A rug was laid out in the open so that Sarat and Ugyen could catch some rest; but the uneven ground, the prickly brambles that pierced through the rugs and crawling insects put paid to the idea. And as if these weren't enough, it began to drizzle. Drenched to their skins, the men were on their feet again before dawn. The route lay along a narrow, slippery track through thick undergrowth in a dark, dripping forest. Lighting a kerosene lamp, Sarat walked on the heels of Phurchung, his shotgun tied to the load the latter was carrying. When they finally set foot in the Rammam Valley, after a few tumbles in the slush, a pale blue dawn was breaking.

The river Rammam marked the boundary of British India. Crossing a flimsy footbridge made of bamboo and weighed down with boulders, Sarat Chandra put on a Tibetan dress. They had now entered the kingdom of Sikkim. Thick forests of saal clothed the hillside, patched up with plots of cotton and cardamom with bamboo watch-stands upon them. The jungles on the upper reaches had turned dark brown in winter. A group of twenty men laden with baskets of oranges were tramping down the winding path; they were heading to the Darjeeling bazaar. Seeing men on ponies, and the gun with them, they respectfully stepped out of the way.

The path now wound up through terraced paddy fields and villages of newly settled farmers. When they reached the top of a ridge after an ascent of several hills, it was late in the afternoon. There was a chorten on top, and a moss-covered mendong: a pile of stones etched with the mantra 'Om mani padme hum'. The place was aptly named Chorten Gong. Behind these stone monuments, a purling stream rolled down to meet the river below. The valley of Daramdin loomed downriver to the south, its emerald paddy fields and thatched cottages gilded by the rays of the setting sun.

'Let's pitch camp here,' Phurchung said. He managed to get fresh vegetables from a Limbu settlement below, and two bottles of millet beer.

Next day the forest grew more luxuriant, with thick clumps of cane and tree ferns. A pall of thick fog and the purl of springs. The path climbed uphill under the canopy of giant oaks and pines festooned with climbers. An hour's climb took them to a place called Rishi Chorten. Here, too, was an ancient mendong. The saddle of the mountain at Hi La presented the sweeping view of south-western Sikkim: the peaks of Tonglu, Singli and even the Darjeeling spur. The jungle was teeming with monkeys and the undergrowth crisscrossed with the tracks of wild boar. The top of the pass was marked with a lap-tse, a pile of stones with reeds stuck into them. At 1 in the afternoon the party reached the level top of the ridge, at a height of 6,000 feet. They forded a number of shallow streams and came to some empty cowsheds. Sarat wanted to take a little rest here but swarming leeches chased him out.

The descent began at 4 o'clock, through clumps of dwarf bamboo, some of which had pieces of red cloth tied on top. Phurchung stood before one and chanted a prayer to the mountain gods. A forest clearing was chosen for the night's halt under the outstretched branches of an ancient oak tree. Here the porters gathered a type of nettle with which they prepared an excellent soup.

Near the Darjeeling railway station, the Hill Cart Road takes a sharp turn before it enters the town's teeming heart. Here the tourist-filled vehicles from the plains would slow down and the booking agents of cheap hotels would jump onto their footboards. They'd cling on to the moving vehicles, thrust their heads into the windows and chant—'Hotel chaiye, hotel?' They'd flash printed brochures and continue—'Hello Sir! Very cheap! Hot water! Best Kanchenjunga view!' This area is known as Lhasa Villa. In the 1990s this was an unremarkable urban sprawl where drivers, automobile mechanics and other low-wage workers lived.

My housemaid stayed in Lhasa Villa. Every year I'd have one or two boys in my class from Lhasa Villa. They would drop out mid-session and join a motor garage or take up a sales job. They pronounced the name of the neighbourhood as a single word. The signboards on the shops there, too, were written that way: Lhasavilla. After I heard it from Lopsang Norbu lips, the place appeared to me for the first time in two separate words.

A village, Norbu had said. But in reality Lhasa Villa was a dingy slum of the kind one saw on the outskirts of any Indian town. But perhaps this really had been a sleepy hamlet a hundred years ago. The imported Japanese pines were yet to rule the skyline, the tea gardens were not so rife, one could still see around the town maples and birches studded with orchids. There was the fear of leopards at dusk, townspeople scarcely ventured this far beyond the railway station. And here, in a nook in the mountain, swaddled in solitude and the call of crickets, a thin settlement had come up around a villa. Twice a day, the solitude would be broken by the whistle of a tiny train negotiating the bend.

But it was impossible to find a shred of that imagined picture on a grey May afternoon in the late 20th century. A pebbled pathway squeezed down between structures of concrete and tin standing cheek by jowl, lines of washings, zinnias and pansies in black plastic bags cast out on narrow railings and squash creepers entwined in the plastic water pipes overhead. Seeing me, a dog chained to a doorpost barked, a white lace curtain on a window was drawn, a woman with a pink towel wrapped around her head cast suspicious glances. A bare-chested young man was bathing a motorbike with soap water; a tattooed scorpion shivered on his shoulder blade. I asked him the direction to Lhasa Villa.

'But this is Lhasavilla!' he said, flashing bad teeth and a wry smile. 'This whole place is Lhasavilla.'

After some more searching I found it at last, lost behind a knot of tenements, the small century-old building designed like a European cottage. It sat on a narrow strip of lawn, enveloped in fog like a blur of memory. A stunted old camellia tree stood in a corner, its branches covered in thick layers of greenish yellow moss.

The building had suffered damage in the great Assam earthquake of 1950. But the scars were indistinguishable from other signs of disrepair. The plaster on the walls had fallen off in places, exposing blocks of rubble held together by wooden frames; rust had eaten away patches of the tin roof; the carved wooden gables had mostly rotted off. But, surprisingly, smoke curled up the broken chimney and folded into the fog. I noticed old newspapers pasted over missing window panes and a TV antenna on the roof. A middle-aged man in shorts opened the door. Both his arms were covered in soap suds; he'd been washing clothes.

The man, a clerk in an insurance company, was a tenant. He had been staying in this cottage for the last three years. The landlord lived in Kathmandu and came once a month to collect the rents. Once upon a time this cottage had belonged to a Bengali. He knew only this much. A journalist from Delhi had visited it the previous year. The man lived alone in a small portion of the building, the rest of it had been turned over to decay. He invited me in warily. In the ancient semi-darkness, heavy with the smell of rotten wood, pale light entering through a skylight lit up a patch of the lichen-spotted wall; damp floorboards gave way under the feet like quicksand. Washings hung on a round wire cage open in the middle, with a glowing brazier inside, from which smoke was rising.

Outside, a light breeze was blowing, churning the grey fog over the ravine, where a stand of cryptomeria pines was slowly drifting into view. Suddenly I understood why Sarat Chandra Das had chosen this particular spot to build this cottage at a time when land was aplenty in the heart of town. Lhasa Villa sat right on the crest of a spur, facing north. On a clear day, the entire range of Kanchenjunga would be visible, like a frozen wave across the sky, as Sarat had first viewed it from Kurseong.

The land of his dreams lay beyond the mountain range, and the fabled city, Lhasa, across forbidding glaciers and valleys. Sarat Chandra had spent half a lifetime here, deciphering arcane manuscripts and lost sutras that he'd brought back.

As he pored over the old brittle papers and palm leaves day after day, didn't his eyes sometimes stray to the range of mountains beyond the windows? Didn't those days of travel in dangerous country, disguised in a lama's garb, in rain that caused deathly chills, the blisters and insect bites, the nights inside yak-hair tents and herdsmen's sheds, the patter of snow on rhododendron bushes and the smell of damp earth, didn't these and other memories return to colour his reveries?

Masses of fog were rising from the khud to cast a haze over the decayed cottage. I tried to conjure up the image of an old man dozing on a lounge chair on the narrow veranda. Instead, there appeared in my mind a young man of twenty-nine, the one who had sneaked out of the town late on a winter night.

Night after night, the enchanting narrative of his journey would keep me tied to my table and open a vista in my own dull uneventful life in the hill town. Reading him, I, too, would feel the breathless climb along a steep slippery path, the heat from the wax lamp in the evening tent, the sour taste of millet beer, the smell of smoke from juniper wood, the nocturnal orchestra of insects, the muffled voices seeping out of the porters' tent into the endless forest night. I'd find my feelings cast like a Brocken Spectre upon the hope and despair of a young man who'd lived a century before me. As the night deepened, the hillside wall of my room would exhale a vegetative breath and the faint gurgle of subterranean springs. I'd look up from the pages to the window. A few sleepless lights of the town would flicker on the dark hillside. The light inside the room would attract a swarm of moths upon the window panes, their resplendent wings spread against glass. A young man's face would appear there, turned towards me, his profile lit up by the table lamp. Before him would also be an open book.

'What are you reading?' I'd ask him.

He would smile and pick up the book, a thick volume bound in cherry-red leather with gilt lettering on it.

The Little Green Girl

Neither the dress nor the physical features of the family squatting on the pavement of Park Street provided any clue to their whereabouts. Only the empty, slightly dazed look on their faces seemed to suggest that they were new to this city. Their ragged belongings, mostly cloth bundles and a couple of rusted tin boxes, were heaped against the Corporation railing. One of the men slept soundly on the kerbstones with a rag over his face; a pair of women sat face to face on their haunches, picking lice from each other's hair; two skinny children were playing with pieces of thermocol. Behind them was the heavy iron gate of the old Christian cemetery; a broad shaded walkway led to the ancient graves. A caretaker was dozing on a stool in the portico, lulled by the cool air. Following days of relentless heat, Kolkata had received a brief squall in the afternoon.

It was the month of April. On a day like this more than two centuries ago, a young Englishman had been felled by a mysterious fever, probably malaria. He was lying somewhere inside the cemetery, in the forest of gothic, baroque and neo-classical memorials built between the late 18th and early 19th centuries. The dates etched on stone said that the majority of the dead were young, and men. There were a few young women too, and also children. Most of them were officers of the East India Company and their families. The fluted sandstone memorials crowned with urns belonged to high-ranking military officers.

A sarcophagus with the relief of a ship's anchor declared that its occupant was taking his final rest after steering his vessel through countless storm-tossed seas. A number of cenotaphs were shaped like hearses, giving them the look of palanquins being carried by invisible bearers. The most celebrated grave in this ancient cemetery, however, belonged to neither a soldier nor an officer, but to a firebrand teacher and poet who had died at the age of twenty-two. He was Henry Vivian Derozio, and he had started a radical movement of English-educated young Bengali men of Calcutta. A cobbled path led to his modest grave. Next to it were a couple of huge, pyramidal obelisks. These were the oldest, built during the 1750s, when there was no dearth of space here. On a lane that went around the pyramids, lost behind double rows of cenotaphs, there was a low, bare, unremarkable grave at plot number 1445A. The white marble plaque had turned grey and was cracked in the middle, but the letters etched on it could still be read:

IN SINCERE ATTACHMENT
To the Memory of
Mr George Bogle
Late Ambassador to Tibet
Who died the 3rd April 1781
This MONUMENT is erected
by his most Affectionate Friends
David Anderson & Claud Alexander

Compared to the florid epitaphs around, it was starkly spare, and as out of place here as the grave itself. There was no mention of the date of birth. Clearly, it was unknown. The bold lettering of 'sincere attachment' and 'monument' suggested that death occurred in an alien city thousands of miles away from home and family, and that the last rites were performed at the initiative of the two friends. In 1781 there were not many memorials around here, shady trees and bushes covered the ground. It was the 3rd of April, a day like this, the beginning of the summer season.

Pale green mango blossoms torn off by the storm lay scattered about the grave, a smell of wet earth filled the air. A pair of grey plovers hopped around in search of worms. A young couple, walking hand in hand, sidled away behind a cenotaph. Tall skyscrapers loomed against the sky like a mirage, across the muted hum of traffic on the busy thoroughfare. It suddenly struck me that the low unadorned grave resembled a mendong. The alphabets which appear on a Mani, representing the mantra 'Om mani padme hum' are usually carved on a mendong, but here it was blank and spattered with moss. Without a thought, I began to circumambulate the grave and came behind it. Something stirred at the sound of my footsteps: it was the pair of children I had seen on the footpath outside. They crouched under a tree and stared at me; they had large white eyes, too large for the skeletal faces in which they were set. They were eating the pale green mango blossoms strewn on the grass.

In 1770, a great famine was sweeping across Bengal, millions were dying of hunger. The Nawab of Bengal's rule had ended only a few years earlier and the East India Company had captured power in the province. Farmers were reeling under the new and punishing tax regime of the Company, the distribution system had collapsed, and a severe drought worsened the situation. A young Company clerk, the son of a Glasgow merchant, arrived in

Calcutta in these desperate times. His name was George Bogle. In the city, however, he was spared the horrors of the famine. The railways were still far away in time, the roads were almost non-existent; the waves of famished humans from the villages hadn't hit the city streets as they would during later famines. But news was pouring in. By the middle of that year, large parts of the Company-ruled districts had turned into veritable burial grounds. In late September, George was writing to his father that 'a million and a half of people are said to have famished in the provinces that belong to the English'. In the villages people were eating wild leaves, they were breaking taboos to eat the meat of dead animals; some were even eating human flesh. But what he'd found particularly shocking—and this would become a pattern in the series of famines that'd follow during the entire British rule—was that people were dying of hunger quietly, without the slightest resistance, without any effort to obtain food by force or other means.

The life of a salaried Company clerk was not cosy in those days. Calcutta was practically a clutch of bungalows and garden houses encircled by the 'black town', the native quarters, made up of slushy dirt roads, thatched huts and fetid bogs teeming with mosquitoes and deadly tropical germs. It was not yet the majestic city of palaces it would become by the middle of the 19th century. Everywhere were scenes of disorder and anarchy under the new Company rule.

That picture began to change when Warren Hastings became the Governor General and took a firm grip on the administration, initiating radical reforms. During this time, George Bogle was made an Assistant Secretary in the Board of Revenue. It didn't take long for the Governor General to take notice of this intelligent young officer. The British East India Company had considerable business interests in China then. The bulk of trade was done along the sea route and via the Canton port, where the Chinese emperor had absolute control. The Company had to pay heavy taxes; moreover, the emperor had banned the import of opium from Bengal into the port city. The only alternative before the Company was to open a land route across Tibet.

Since the middle ages, Tibet had a central place in the map of commerce that extended from the coast of Bay of Bengal to China, Persia, the land of the Tartars and even Siberia. Tibetan merchants sold Chinese silk, paper, horses, musk, yak tails, sheep and gold; the export items from this side included muslin, glass, corals, pearls, spices, camphor and betel leaves. This little-known land across the Himalaya, known to India as Bhot, hadn't yet closed its doors to foreigners. Warren Hastings sent George Bogle to the court of the Panchen Lama in Shigatse as the ambassador of the East India Company, with the intention of opening a monopoly trade link.

Among the many tasks that Hastings had assigned his deputy, the most important was to examine the nature of the roads between the borders of Bengal and Lhasa. Bogle was directed to keep a detailed record of his observations of the people, their manners and customs, trade and commerce, administration and revenue system, as well as the climate, roads, house designs and cuisine. He was given a bag of potato seeds that he was supposed to plant in the settlements along his route. Finally, he was handed a list of items that he was supposed to bring back from Tibet. The list included, among other things, seeds of valuable and curious plants like walnut, rhubarb, ginseng; and pairs of animals called tiss, which produced shawl wool, and cattle, whose tails were used as fly whisks. The animals were to be brought back live—by dooley, chair or any other contrivance.

George Bogle set out from Calcutta in May 1774. He was twenty-eight.

May was scorching in the plains of Bengal, and Bogle mostly travelled at night to escape the heat. It took him a fortnight to reach the kingdom of Cooch Behar, the northernmost part of Bengal, by boat and on horseback. From there he pressed on further north, to a territory on which no Company servant had set foot before—terra incognita. He was accompanied by Dr. Hamilton, an assistant surgeon, and a small group of porters.

Endless marshes began. The path entered thickets of tall grass and reeds. It buzzed with the sounds of frogs and insects, and the air was so damp that it seemed like the lungs filled up with water at every breath. After 12 miles appeared a forest of saal and other tall trees. A river flowed round it, forming a natural boundary between Cooch Behar and the kingdom of Bhutan. Bogle and his party crossed the stream in a dug-out canoe and stepped into the foot of a chain of hills that marked the frontier of Bengal. Tibet lay beyond the hills. They passed a derelict fort that bore signs of recent ravage and ended the day's march in a small village.

The night's halt was arranged at the headman's hut, made of bamboo and thatched with leaves, raised from the ground on stilts. The walls and the floor inside were woven with reeds, without any iron or ropes; it resembled a bird cage. A notched tree trunk served as a staircase. Half a dozen men from the village were gathered inside; they consumed a bottle of rum and got drunk in no time. A peddler woman, shapely and with a fine set of teeth, was staying with the headman. Bogle noted that she had eyes like the wife of the famous Flemish painter, Rubens. Dressed in a single shawl pinned at the shoulder with a silver brooch, her fine legs bared up to her knees, she drank freely with the men. At night the men and the woman went to sleep in a confused heap on the floor.

Bogle and his men set out at daybreak. Now they advanced towards the tall range of mountains that had been looming in the horizon for the past few days like a battlement. The forest grew dense and crowded with giant saals, clear streams meandered through it upon beds of smooth pebbles. The path grew rugged and when they finally reached the foothills, it was 2 in the afternoon. A bridle path wound gently up through the dark forest to a certain height, then the ascent became steep. The path tapered off to a trail and ascended up the mountain for about 4 miles, across springs cascading down the cliffs. The climb continued until shadows thickened in the forests and the murmuring waters exhaled a scented breath. It was almost evening when Bogle reached Buxa subah, an outpost of Cooch Behar State abutting the kingdom of Bhutan.

Buxa sat on top of a hill, with mountains rising behind it like giant ocean waves. A narrow dell lay below, bordered with a low wall of loose stones and an ancient banyan with outstretched branches. The Dewan of Buxa subah came next morning to offer a ceremonial welcome to the officer of the East India Company. He brought as gifts a white scarf, butter, rice and tea leaves. A long and difficult journey lay ahead. They spent the next day in Buxa and recruited more porters to carry the luggage uphill.

On 9th June George Bogle ventured into the dark green mountains of Bhutan. He was riding a scrawny but sure-footed pony. Now he was beyond the Company's jurisdiction, but he had a passport of the Rajah of Cooch Behar. As the party pushed onto the Pichakonum mountain that loomed over Buxa, the path became truly forbidding. Narrow, steep, and paved with uneven slabs of bastard marble, it hugged the sheer mountainside. But the scary aspect of the high precipices was mitigated by dark green forest cover. By mid-afternoon, the party scaled the top of the first of a series of mountain ranges. It was the height of summer, but the air was pleasantly cool. Bogle stood upon the crest of the ridge and, before beginning the descent to the other side, cast a last look in the direction of Bengal.

The change of terrain was so abrupt, the contrast so stark, that it took away the young Scotsman's breath. The weather was clear to the south, the eye travelled unhindered across the endless plains. Not a hill or a rise, no tower or hump, but miles upon miles of amazingly flat plains stitched with forests, farmlands and grazing grounds, hazy lines of rivers and clusters of villages with threads of smoke curling up to the skies.

But what really stole the heart of the young Scotsman was the view on the other side, the one that lay before him: steep descents, deep glens, giant trees holding up the skies like cathedral columns, and mountains piled on mountains, their crowns lost in the clouds.

In Ritwik Ghatak's film *Komal Gandhar*, a young man grows ecstatic when he has a clear view of the flat plains of Bengal from the heights of Kurseong and exclaims to a friend: 'Have you seen the plains of Bengal? When there's no cloud, it seems as if a little green girl is lying there, smiling sweetly.'

On the way to Darjeeling along the Hill Cart Road, after the first ascent from the Terai, the traveller would look back from an unforgettable village named Rongtong in the direction of the south and have this view of the endless flat plains. I still remember that moment from many years ago, when I was going to Darjeeling to join my new job. It was the season of the rains. The teak plantations of the Sukna range below were in bloom, the forest canopy was dusted with pale green blossoms. Siliguri town lay beyond it in a steaming haze. The road wound up the dark green mountains whose crests were lost in charcoal clouds.

Such moments, and the feelings of vague anxiety and hope that cling to them, are stored in memory in the shape of an image. Sarat Chandra Das went to Darjeeling more than a century before me. What were his feelings when he cast a last look back at the endless plains? Was he, like George Bogle, captivated by the lofty, cloud-scarfed mountains? Or did he, a son of the Gangetic plains, find himself glancing back at the unbelievably flat plains of Bengal that lay beyond the belt of forests, like a little green girl sweetly smiling?

George Bogle had started his journey from Calcutta in May and reached Tashilhunpo in December. He had stayed there till the end of winter. During this time he had become a good friend of the Panchen Lama, and, as an ambassador of the East India Company, had worked towards opening a trade route through Bhutan. These were remarkable achievements, and the

Company was planning to send him again to Tibet to finalize the agreements. The Panchen Lama had gone to China, and it was decided that Bogle would meet up with him there and they would return together to Tibet. But the great lama contracted smallpox and died in Beijing. A few months later, on 3 April 1781, George Bogle died of tropical fever in Calcutta.

In 1788 the Gorkhas invaded Tibet, the monastery at Tashilhunpo was plundered and valuable books and manuscripts were destroyed. Tibet finally managed to drive out the Gorkhas with the help of China. The East India Company, already a major player in the power game of this region, did nothing. This effectively sealed the fate of a friendship between Tibet and British India. The mountain passes leading into Tibet were closed to outsiders, and would remain so for more than a century until Francis Younghusband led a military expedition there in 1903.

Following Warren Hastings' advice, George Bogle had kept a detailed journal of his visit to Tibet. After his death, this journal was sent back to Britain along with his personal belongings. For nearly a hundred years, it was lost inside a wooden chest, amid a pile of letters and documents, in a country villa in Scotland. The geographical department of the India Office finally laid their hands on this journal and published it in 1875, together with the account of another traveller to Tibet, Thomas Manning, the first Englishman to visit Lhasa in 1811.

When Sarat Chandra Das came to Darjeeling as the headmaster of the Bhutia Boarding School, the Deputy Commissioner, John Edgar, lent him this book. Was it part of a larger design? This can never be known. The book, newly published in London, was a large volume bound in cherry-red

Morocco leather, with gilt lettering on it. It stirred up in the young Bengali schoolmaster a deep curiosity for the forbidden land on the roof of the world.

Darjeeling, too, was a young town then; a scattering of tin-roofed wooden cottages and cobbled paths winding around them. All the paths led to a road, the Cart Road, which brought the visitors from the hot plains on ponies and palanquins. The goods were carried up on buffalo carts, the somnolent groan of whose wooden axles roused the tiny bazaar. A short ramble out of the town led to pristine forests. Local hunters brought fabulous birds and animals from there, both live and stuffed, to sell in the bazaar. Day after day, the Himalaya laid out its magical wonders before the eyes of the young Bengali. To the north, veiled in clouds or resplendent in the rays of the sun, loomed the Kanchenjunga. After he read the book of Bogle's travels, Sarat had this burning desire to follow the path across the mountains.

Ugyen Gyatso, the lama from the Rinchenpong monastery in Sikkim, had then joined the school as his assistant. He belonged to the Gelug Pa or Yellow Hat sect affiliated to Tashilhunpo. Sarat persuaded Ugyen to obtain for him a passport to Tibet. Expectedly, it didn't take long for the British government to give the go-ahead. Things were falling into place, as in a jigsaw puzzle.

Rinchen Tenwa

11 November, morning. The sky was partly clouded and there was rain and sunshine. The raindrops glittered in the sun and fell silently, like flaming flowers, into the ravines. Hi was a quiet village of Lepchas and Limbus; the latter grew paddy on stepped fields and seemed quite well-off. There were fenced plots of cardamom above the swift-flowing Kalai, or Kalhait. The river originated near the Singli Pass, meandered for about 20 miles and debouched into the Rangeet. Villages stood along the banks, upon ridges, under lofty trees above the steep hillsides. Fish were plentiful in the stream and well-known for their taste, which the Limbu inhabitants caught in the shallows with bamboo nets lined with the leaves of a toxic plant.

Sarat and his men took the path that left the river and wound uphill through thickets of reed and tall grass. It was the habitat of wild boars and porcupines. After about 3,000 feet of steady ascent, Pemyangshe, Yantang and other villages appeared into view upon the distant flat ridges. On the right, set amidst orange orchards and fields of millet, was a hamlet called Lingcham. The night halt was arranged in a Limbu house here.

The ascent continued the next day along a trail that led through fields of maize and derelict Limbu cottages. A lone woman plodding with a basket of wild apricots passed them. At 2 in the afternoon the party reached the top of the ridge and took the path around a moss-lined chorten. The monastery of

Sanga Choeling loomed on their right, on the brow of the ridge. Now the path cut through underbrush and nettles in a dense forest of oaks and pines, and when they reached Taley, the day was drawing to a close.

Taley was a settlement of twenty houses. Tranquil horses and cows were grazing around the homestead land. Seeing wayfarers, the villagers came out and begged for salt in exchange for chhang, the rice beer. The salt traders from Yampung hadn't come this way because of early snowfall. But Sarat's party didn't have enough salt to spare. Next day, the men and animals followed the Ringbi for about 5 miles along a circuitous trail, crossing and re-crossing the stream over bamboo bridges below the village of Nambura. By now the path had grown narrow and slippery as it gained height, and was cut into a steep cliff face. They had to step carefully over fissured rocks, clutching on to creepers and clumps of grass. A few hundred feet below, the torrent boiled and foamed, stones loosened by the hooves of ponies fell like feathers into its raging mouth. The stream had cut a deep gully across a huge boulder, with a wooden ladder laid over it. In a fissure of rock, Sarat spotted a red Tibetan shirt and a few stuffed pheasants. These birds sometimes turned up at the bazaar in Darjeeling, he remembered.

They camped in Ringbi, a tiny settlement of six cottages on a flat mountain terrace. It commanded a superb view: craggy cliffs rising behind them and across the deep gorge cut by the river, thick forests of oak, pine, wild plantain and giant rattan creepers hanging from ancient trees. No sooner had they reached the spot than Phurchung dropped his load and ran off to an acquaintance's house to buy beer for his master. He returned with three bottles tucked under his arms, one of which was rightfully his.

The tent was pitched on a grassy flat above the river, a rug was spread inside it. As Sarat stretched upon it and sipped the beer, he could feel the fatigue of the trek ebbing away from his limbs. The porters were on their own; some had gone to the forest to collect firewood, or to pick wild edible herbs, others to the village to buy provisions. Not a sound could be heard except for the rush of torrents in the gorge below. As Sarat sank into sleep, his mind shut off the past and opened out to a future filled with anticipation.

The morning was clear and offered a majestic view of the mountains. But Phurchung was nowhere to be found. He had been sent the day before to a village around the ridge to stock up rations before the difficult crossing that lay ahead. Sarat waited for him till mid-morning before calling off the day's march. Phurchung returned in the afternoon, sozzled, but his mission accomplished. He had collected rice, maize, eggs, vegetables and a live lamb. After profuse salaaming and the contrite rolling of his tongue in Tibetan fashion, he withdrew from sight.

At Ringbi, too, the villagers asked for salt; in exchange they wanted to barter a type of wild creeper that produced red dye.

'Don't go any further! The passes are closed, there's a fresh snowfall,' they warned.

Now Sarat was in a bind. They could stay back for some more time in the village because food was available there. But what if the news reached the Tibetan border guards? Also, the pass was still four days' march away. How would they know when the snow would melt? Finally, the party took another route to cross the range over the Yampung La pass, which was still open. They passed themselves off as shikaris out on a hunting trip, and assured the villagers that they wouldn't need to go over the pass. The shotgun and belt of cartridges slung across Phurchung's back did help.

Tall cypresses appeared beyond Ringbi, and an ancient juniper tree with vast outstretched branches. Soon they came to a cavernous hollow under a huge boulder, which the locals called 'dechan fug', the cavern of bliss and the haunt of demigods. The path was now easy along the bank, with steps cut into rock at places and cane bridges across the springs cascading into the river. They saw Limbu men weaving bamboo mats and collecting willow shoots to thatch their huts. At 1 o'clock the party reached Paongtang and camped in a tumbledown dong-khang, a rest shed for travellers. It was so cramped and low that a man could scarcely stand upright. After the cooking-fire was lit and the bellows worked, the place was choking with smoke and dust, and crawling with centipedes. But the coolies wouldn't pitch the tents they were carrying. Since a dong-khang was around, why shouldn't it be put to good use? they argued. And then, as if there wasn't enough misery, it began to drizzle.

But dinner was on time, and there was excellent fish. It turned out that a cousin of Phurchung was a herdsman who lived in a neighbouring village; he had helped them get milk, cheese, beer and the fish. After the beer took care of the fatigue, it was time for music. A pair of coolies, Jordan and Tonzang, sang. Although they did the job of common porters, they were respected men in this region. They had been drafted to ensure a smooth passage through the villages on the way.

Sarat was deeply moved after he witnessed how a few drops

of liquor and simple folk tunes in the solitude of the mountains uncovered glimpses of a rich, ancient culture. The two men sang from a popular ballad cycle called *Rinchen Tenwa*, the precious rosary.

The *Rinchen Tenwa* is a collection of ballads that has remained alive in the memories of the Himalayan people for hundreds of years. Sakya Pandit, who went to Tashilhunpo from India in the 13th century, translated this Tibetan ballad cycle into Sanskrit. In the early 19th century, the Hungarian scholar Csoma de Koros translated parts of it into English. The ballad is still alive in the hills of Sikkim, in Lepcha, Limbu and other languages.

More than a hundred years after Sarat Chandra heard strains of the *Rinchen Tenwa* in a herdsman's shed in Ringbi, I heard them on a trek inside the Singalila National Park from the lips of a blind singer. His name was Purba and he was travelling with us in the company of porters. He had with him a sarangi, a short-necked string instrument carved out of a single piece of wood.

From the Barshey Valley in west Sikkim on the way to Kalijar was a dry lake known as Deoningalo Dhap. Its saucer-shaped bed was fed by the runoff from gentle slopes that ringed it. But in March the water had drained away and the ground was covered with clumps of dry yellow grass. Our tents were pitched along the edge of the lake, on thick carpets of grass, below a grove. Thickets of slender bamboos abounded here, which the locals called deoningalo, sacred bamboo, and collected them as charms to keep in their homes. Forests of magnolias and rhododendrons covered the upper part of the mountains. It was spring, and the trees were in bloom. The pink and scarlet flowers appeared to be drifting in swirls of soupy grey fog when we reached there in the afternoon. But after the sun set, a breeze began and soon the sky was polished clean. The cold, too, became sharp. We built a fire of deadwood scavenged from the lake bed. To prevent the sparks from flying around and into the dry grass, we stood shoulder to shoulder, forming a wall against the wind. Purba sat across us, near the fire, and sang with passion.

All here assembled, pray listen with attention—
The eagle is the king of all birds. When he rises, all rise.
The lion is the king of beasts. When he leaps, all leap.
And he who drinks is the prince of speech. When he speaks, all listen.

He sat on a packing box, with folded knees and the sarangi pressed against his cheek. The deep lines on his face appeared to be pulsing in the glow from the fire. Sometimes the force of the music pushed his face up to the sky, the flaring sparks gleamed on his pale, sightless eyeballs and on the miniscule knife sewn on to his black topi. Long after we had retreated to the tents and into our sleeping bags, snatches of music were still coming from the mess tent. It ebbed and lost itself among the tinkle of yak bells. The huge hairy animals carried our luggage in the daytime, at night they were set free near the tents.

There was an elderly Canadian in our group, a retired professor of Sociology. When someone told him the gist of the lyric Purba was singing, he narrated to us a ritual practised by a Pacific island tribe to select their chief. The aspirants would be made to sit in a circle, with a pot of wine in the middle, and all the members of the tribe would gather around them. The contestants would take sips from the pot of wine and pass it around, and confer about the welfare of the tribe and their habitat. The pot would be filled continually. The one who managed to sit through till the end, talk coherently and drink the wine following the right etiquette, would be elected chief.

For long, the forests, valleys, cliffs and waterfalls of this region, recorded in such vivid detail in the writings of Joseph Dalton Hooker and Sarat Chandra Das, had been fermenting in my mind. During my years in Darjeeling, when the monsoon season stretched on for months and a leaden light deranged the hours of the day, when dark feelings sprouted in the recesses of the mind like hallucinogenic mushrooms, I tried to recall those wooded mountains and valleys that a young man from my city had traversed a century ago. I'd wait for opportunities to slip out and follow the so-called Hooker's Trails around the town.

Hooker had come to the Darjeeling hills in 1848. He had travelled to the forests on the Singalila mountain range, climbed up to Dzongri and had briefly entered Tibet through Sikkim and eastern Nepal. Thirty years later Sarat Chandra Das would follow this route. When I visited the region, much of the ancient forests outside the sanctuary had been lost to grazing and step farming. And yet the blue velvety underside of the leaves of the silver fir, the veins of mica upon the gneiss, the first tentative lights of dawn over the snow of Kanchenjunga, the distant call of the golden eagle, the scent of juniper smoke and other wonders that crowded the pages of Hooker's journals had remained.

I got a transfer from Darjeeling and returned to Kolkata. Many years later, I came to know that the Sikkim tourism department was organizing a five-day trek programme in the Singalila National Park. By that time, the memories of my wanderings in that region had bled into my readings of Hooker and Sarat Das. I felt the old yearnings again and so I went to the office of the Sikkim tourism department on Middleton Street. The trek programme was a joint venture of the department and an organization of private tour operators, they told me, in what is fashionably called the PPP (Public Private Partnership) model. Tourists from different parts of the country and abroad were taking part in it.

It was the month of March, the rhododendrons were in bloom, the forests of Singalila were a riot of colours. Sarat Chandra Das had walked in these forests. So had Joseph Dalton Hooker before him.

CROSSINGS

'Soon after this we came to a flat, grass-covered valley with tall rhododendrons and ferns growing about it. Phurchung held this spot to have been a singularly lucky one for him, for it was here that his parents had met Hooker some thirty-five years ago, while the great botanist was exploring Nepal.'

—Sarat Chandra Das, *Journey to Lhasa and Central Tibet*

'A good-looking girl came to ask me for medicine for her husband's eyes, which had suffered from snow-blindness: she brought me a present of snuff, and carried a little child, stark naked, yet warm from the powerful rays of the sun, at nearly 14,000 feet elevation, in December! I prescribed for the man, and gave the mother a bright farthing to hang round the child's neck.'

—Joseph Dalton Hooker, *Himalayan Journals*

An Amulet

To reduce the load before the difficult trek ahead, the tent had been sent back to Darjeeling with Jordan and Tonzang. A night shelter was made with a pair of bedsheets tied to the low branches of trees. It was a deep forest, the habitat of leopards and wild boars. Raw meat and fish were kept tied to the high branch of a chestnut, out of the reach of foraging animals. But the smell attracted owls and rats; the eerie forest night was magnified by their screeches, their scurrying feet and flapping wings.

But the morning turned out bright. Sarat and his men emerged from the forest and saw in the distance the village of Yampung Dok, nestled in a glen. Bathed in the morning sun reflected off the snow, it appeared so clearly, like a painting, that even without field glasses, he could pick out the cottages, the yak sheds and prayer flags lashing the sky. A path threaded around a low mendong before the village. But when they finally reached it in the afternoon, Yampung Dok turned out to be a picture of desolation. Not a living soul was around, except famished crows cawing from flag poles, deepening the sense of gloom. There were a dozen rough cottages made of loose stone slabs with roofs of pine planks held in place by boulders; the doors were secured with ropes. Bales of wild dye-creepers, which they had seen at Ringbi, were stored inside. During the summer, when snow melted over the passes, traders from eastern Nepal would come to barter salt for these plants. Big monoliths were strewn around, encrusted with beehives shaped like mushrooms. The party left the desolate sight and marched to another pass, the Du La. The ascent became steep from here.

Villagers at Ringbi had warned them of an early snowfall. Their warning came true as Sarat pressed on up the rise. There was snow on all sides, and the ridge on the north was slathered with the glacier of the dreaded Kangchan mountain. At Du La, Ugyen showed symptoms of mountain sickness—headache and persistent lack of breath. A wind was blowing over the pass, so fierce that it pulled the men off their feet. A porter tumbled over snow and suffered frost-bite on his feet. Sarat gave him his own shoes and the Kabuli socks he was carrying, and put on new Tibetan boots himself. The path was completely blocked with fresh snow, forcing them to make a detour along the western flank of the pass. Here the snow had hardened, but crevasses lurked at every step. With extreme caution, sometimes crawling on hands and feet, they pressed on like terrified snails until the descent began. After about two hours, deep gorges came into view; they were dotted with tiny pasture lands. The men walked across a bed of glacial moraine and re-entered the treeline.

They reached Gumong-tang in the evening. It was a beautiful place. Grasslands, belts of juniper around bare rock cliffs and, across the gorge, a melting glacier had formed a lake of deep black water. This was known as Lachmi Pokhri, the lake of fortune. The porters said that a herd of water buffaloes lived in its depths, guarding caskets of gems.

The most difficult stage of the journey began the next day, 19th November. The men first forded a knee-deep stream and began to climb up to Bogto La. Again the trail wound up alongside a dry glacier bed, fringed with forests of fir and juniper, and a thin stream flowing down the middle. After some distance the trail forked, a well-worn arm leading up to the only dong-khang on the Bogto slope. Phurchung chose the less trodden one. It was completely desolate because, as Sarat learnt, the salt traders of Yangma avoided it. A type of toxic plant grew on the wayside that could kill pack animals if they nibbled at its leaves. But there were large flocks of pheasants; the birds were pecking at rhododendron berries. They also spotted wild sheep in the distance.

As the climb continued up the bare grey cliff, the rhododendrons and junipers fell away and a moss-like vegetation appeared on the rock faces. The strains of high-altitude climbing now became acute, especially since, for the past few days, the men had been reduced to a diet of rice and tea. The condition of the porters was particularly pitiable. The wind was sharp, dark clouds raced against the sky. The men dragged themselves up the slope in a painfully slow motion. His own head had been aching since morning; now he felt a nausea brewing in the pit of his stomach. He climbed another half mile and fell flat on his face.

It was Phurchung who carried Sarat on his back to the top of the pass. Someone prepared tea, but he could not swallow it. His limbs were numb, and he had a hammering headache. Phurchung coaxed him to eat a frozen egg and some dry fruits. He was swaddled in blankets and his feet propped against the luggage, so that he wouldn't tumble down the steep slope. This way Sarat pulled through the night, without sleep, listening to the rumble of avalanches.

But a more harrowing situation lay in store the next day. The dawn broke on an overcast sky, presaging a snowstorm.

Phurchung, otherwise a jolly, intrepid fellow, was reluctant to advance any further and had to be ordered to advance. He finally set off, but not before chanting some mantras. After a short climb over the snow, the men came to a small oval lake that was completely frozen. The path lay across a series of connected ridges covered with sheets of ice. It was a scene of the wildest grandeur and absolute silence, with not even the sound of an avalanche to disturb it. One by one they tiptoed across the mirror of the frozen lake, following the line of snow that Phurchung left in his wake to mark the path. This was the Tso dom-dongma, the lake of the peacock's spots, with air bubbles trapped under the bluish green surface of ice, giving it the appearance of a spotted peacock's tail.

And just as a dark sky laden with rain-bearing clouds makes the peacock unfurl its tail, the plumage of ice across the lake surface did the reverse: it called up thick clouds from below and cast a veil over the sky. Suddenly the light dimmed. Phurchung went pale with fear.

'Why proceed further up, Sir?' he wailed. 'Death awaits us in this desolate place. One hour more and we shall all be gone.'

Overhead, the massed-up clouds threatened to fall in a shower of snow, massive enough to bury them all.

But Sarat was adamant. There was no point in retreating now, he argued, because if the snow fell in an hour, they'd all be trapped as they had left Bogto La far behind. With unexpected energy and resolve, he now took the lead himself. The men began to move again. In an hour's time, when they'd reached the top of another pass, the clouds had cleared up and a brilliant sun shone in a deep blue sky.

After two days of steady descent, across ridges and rocky cliffs, over fields of snow marked with the footprints of snow leopards, on foot and on Phurchung's back, Pundit Sarat Chandra Das entered the soothing green line of vegetation again. They had reached Kangpa-chan. It was a grassy valley clothed with clumps of rhododendrons and large ferns. Birds were calling in the trees. The place was suffused with a delicate peace. Phurchung kneeled and touched his forehead on the ground. This seemed odd, since neither a shrine nor a sacred stone could be seen anywhere. He also kissed a locket on his neck.

'This place is sacred to my family,' Phurchung explained. 'My father got back his eyesight here. A sahib cured him. That was long time ago, I was this small.'

He held out his hands to indicate the size of a baby; then he took out the necklace with the locket.

'The sahib had given this medal to me,' he said to Sarat, handing him the amulet.

It was a silver farthing, with King George IV's head embossed on it. The year 1842 was etched in Roman numerals.

5 December 1848. A rustle of a snowfall woke Joseph. But when he peeped out of his yak-hair tent, he could only see thick mist. The night before they had camped inside this rhododendron grove; pencils of sun now streamed in through the foliage and banded the mist. And then he saw them: a group of wayfarers moving through the forest. They had sheep, large as mules, with sacks of salt hanging from their backs. The withered leaves being crushed under the hooves of the animals produced the sound of a snowfall. There were men, women and children in the group, Joseph noted, dressed in heavy Tibetan costumes and walking

single file at a steady, languid pace. When an animal stopped to crop the plants growing on the roots of rhododendron trees, one of the women would emit a low whistle to call it back. Other than this, no one made a sound. Wisps of breath smoked from their nostrils and melted into the luminous mist. This appeared like a vision in the pale light of dawn. There were tents inside the forest, but no one stopped or turned to look. All of them had their eyes fixed before them on the path—all except a girl with a baby in her arms. She glanced back furtively and her eyes, gleaming with curiosity, met Joseph's. A pair of thin braids hung, serpent-like, out of her fur cap. As the girl walked away, she looked back a few times. The men and animals receded away into the shadowy grove. Then the fog thinned, the forest came alive with the call of snow pheasants. The birds would come down to the ground at this hour to drink the dew drops on blades of grass. Joseph fell asleep.

He woke up late in the morning. The porters were already up and about. They packed the luggage, rolled up the tents, rustled up some breakfast and the march resumed.

Joseph Dalton Hooker was exploring the Yarlung Valley, across the Chunjarma Pass, collecting plant specimens. Winter had set in, most of the flowering plants above 10,000 feet had dried, the seeds had gone back to sleep in their icy graves. Desiccated stalks of primrose, anemone and potentilla were strewn in the glades over the dry waterbed, under rocks and in shades below the dwarf rhododendrons and junipers. One could imagine how this whole valley would erupt in colours in monsoon. Joseph had with him a complete mobile laboratory equipped with thermometers, microscope, field glasses, compasses of different types, sextant and other surveying instruments, boxes for insects and plant specimens, chemicals to preserve the breath-taking variety of plants, flowers and seeds that grew in this part of the earth. He would be busy collecting during the daytime, on his way from camp to camp, and would devote the long evenings to classification, drawing and note-taking. Inside the yak-hair tent, under dim candlelight, the pages of his notebook would fill up with the details of flora and fauna, aspects of geography, the properties of stones and the climate.

The explorers in the Himalaya would usually set out early in the morning and reach the next campsite before noon, before the weather took a turn. But Joseph did things his own way. He would spend the morning hours, his mind and body refreshed after rest and at their receptive best, around the campsite. Then, after a heavy breakfast, he would continue with the march late in the afternoon, to find his tent pitched and things arranged at the next halting place. His writing and drawing equipment would be neatly laid out on a table made out of packing boxes, with a candle covered in glass to keep out the insects. Under a big tree, the cook would be busy preparing his dinner: usually boiled rice and potatoes, mutton stew, biscuits and tea, with occasional delicacies like tinned truffle and dried dates. He would work through the evening and sometimes late into the night.

That day, late in the morning, a column of moisture-laden clouds formed in the sky. The lonely forest path glowed a magical green under the leaden sky, a pair of golden eagles were circling low under it. It presaged rain. As the Englishman hurried on, the face of a young woman flashed in his mind; it seemed as if he had seen that face in a dream. There was a strange light glinting in her narrow eyes, and she held a pink baby in her arms. By afternoon he left the cloud-capped forest behind and met the group again. They had halted at a clearing on the edge of a forest of tall birches. Tea was boiling over a fire of dried leaves, the sheep were cropping grass. The group was travelling from Wallangchun to Yalung, he learned.

Joseph's men had pitched camp at a nearby spot. Next morning, the girl with the baby came to the tent to beg medicine for her husband who was suffering from snow-blindness. The girl was pretty, Joseph noted, and the baby in her arms was naked, despite the altitude and the cold. She had brought a present of snuff for the sahib. Joseph gave medicine for her husband and a farthing for the baby. The large silver coin brought forth a glow of joy on her face. She had never seen a white man before, and now she began to cast probing glances at Joseph's eyes, hair and skin with frank curiosity. She had also never seen such an array of strange instruments. She lingered inside the tent, inspecting each item with fascination. They didn't share a language, and yet there wasn't a hint of stiffness in her manners.

Joseph beckoned the girl. He pressed the chronometer to her ear and watched the expressions playing on her face. The field glass and the box of insects, too, elicited deep fascination. But things went out of hand when Joseph tried to show her the mechanism of a spring measuring tape. As the steel tape sprang out of its leather pouch with the hiss of a serpent, the mother and the child screamed in terror and they bolted out of the tent.

Joseph Dalton Hooker's clandestine foray into Tibet, despite the resistance from Sikkimese officials and the Tibetan guard commander (who paid with his life for this lapse of duty), was in many ways a breakthrough. Over the next half century, explorers, mystics, spies and a tailor would follow this route. The path Sarat Chandra Das took thirty years later more or less overlapped with Hooker's. These paths went in tandem, sometimes converging and sometimes branching off, like rivers. Rivers of narration, meandering across a map composed of grey rock, water, birdsong, pine cones, snow, sunsets and silences; spaces inscribed with anxiety and ambition, terror and joy.

The deserted village that Sarat had seen at Yampung Dok was, although smaller in size, a mirror image of the one Joseph had visited in the Yangma Valley. It nestled at 14,000 feet upon a narrow stone terrace. A collection of rickety stone huts plastered with yak dung huddled between huge boulders that had rolled down with avalanches in prehistoric times. There was a row of squat chortens before the village, fluttering prayer flags, and upon the slopes tiny farm plots fenced with stones.

The Yangma Valley bifurcated from here: one broad arm went to the snow-covered mountains to the north-east, the other towards Kangchen Pass on the west. The rock faces were bare and rugged since no tree would grow at this height. On all sides were moraines left behind by glaciers, grey green plants on dry lake beds and huge blocks of stone. Snow-clad mountains towered around. Altogether a rugged scene, Joseph noted, it was sublime and wonderful.

The village appeared like a mirage, without a hint of life. The men pitched the tents below it, on a plot of dry-stubble land. Next morning Joseph went to explore the village, to find its inhabitants bracing for the long winter. The fields had been harvested and the grains stored, the firewood collected from the forests below, chopped and stacked in piles, the cheese made and dried. The passes were closed under heavy snow and the ground was frozen as hard as flint. The cottages clustered like a beehive, with narrow alleys threading between them. Tiny vents under roofs exhaled smoky air on the face of the inquisitive Englishman and suffused him with a yeasty smell. The lower floors were half-buried in the ground, where firewood, yak dung and wool were stored. Step ladders led up to low, narrow living quarters. Daylight never entered there, the soot-blackened rooms were illuminated by braziers. Shadowy humans huddled there. They dozed, spun wool and told prayer beads on slow fingers. This way they would spend the four long months of winter, while outside a deathly silence would reign. Only the yaks would be out under the open skies, their shaggy backs encrusted with snow, their bells rattling as long as traces of green remained in the cracks of stones. Before the fleeting daylight would fade, women with wooden tubs would crawl out of the cottages and call the animals in. For a while, the slopes would come alive with shrill human voices and deep bovine grunts answering them. And then, as the temperature would plummet further, milk would freeze in the yaks' udders, the mountain springs would freeze like candle drippings, the rumble of avalanches would echo in the deathly silence. On clear nights countless stars, pulsating and large, would transform the sky into the coat of a snow leopard in flight.

The Lost Village

One hundred and fifty years after Joseph Hooker had set foot in these mountains, we found the remains of a village in Kalijar, inside the Singalila National Park. It appeared as if a ruined village had sunk into the earth; only the foundations and a couple of stone walls remained standing. Old hearth fires had left layers of soot on the stone, and there were splotches of grime overlaid with greenish orange lichens; without them, one could easily have mistaken the piles of stone for some sort of a shrine.

At 12,000 feet, Kalijar was a narrow notch between a pair of humps. We found the remains near our campsite. Topless trunks of pines and silver firs stood against the slopes, damaged by storm or lightning; from a distance, they appeared like the broken columns of a lost city. The top of Phokte rose another 1,000 feet from there.

'Take a good look at the summit before the light goes. We'll climb there early in the morning tomorrow. All the famous peaks in this part of the Himalayas can be viewed from the top.' Dr. Joshi, our team leader, announced.

It was late afternoon, a pall of fog hung all around us. Team members were emerging from it in small groups, exhausted after the day-long trek.

'I guess there'll be snowfall in the evening,' Joshi remarked, the vertical line on his brow deepening with anxiety.

He began to clap and barked orders at the porters in Nepali

and the men ran about pell-mell to pitch the tents. Some of them climbed down to a nearby spring to collect water. The yaks had been set free, their leather harnesses, ropes, sacks of provisions and cooking utensils were heaped against a boulder. Purba the singer sat amid the clutter and fiddled his sarangi distractedly. Noodle soup bubbled in a large pot. The warm scent emanating from it unleashed pangs of hunger. Tired and famished, we stretched out on the cold coppery grass like logs, or took off our shoes and attended to the blisters on our feet. A few of us moved about listlessly and explored the campsite.

Behind the remains of a hutment I found a piece of rotted bamboo matting which, once upon a time, must have been part of a ceiling or a partition wall. Years of weathering had turned it black, an inextricable part of the flagstone on which it lay, the weave mimicking the texture of metamorphic rock.

It was a clear sunny morning when we'd set off for Kalijar. The rhododendrons and magnolias were in full bloom, and bathed in the dazzling sun against a blinding blue sky. Cobalt sunbirds were fluttering around the blossoms and making split-second darts at them. When they dived into the stamens, their tiny bodies completely disappeared inside the flowers. Pink, crimson and pale white petals lay strewn on grass. In the mountains, white magnolias were in bloom. From a distance, they appeared like stars which had dropped from the sky at night and had gotten stuck on the leafless branches.

The second day's campsite was a broad glen called Thulo Dhap, the big step. A shallow stream flowed over it, around stands of tall rhododendrons with bright red flowers. Beyond the stream, a trail wound steeply up. We had to ford the stream to reach the foot of the trail.

Pasang, the leader of the coolie gang, turned to us and declared: 'Agari bato dherai ukalo cha! Pura garh-fataunu!'

For the benefit of the foreigners in the group, he translated: 'Bato meaning track, ukalo is steep and garh-fataunu is...' He touched his own buttocks with both hands and clapped noisily. That was translation enough.

A punishing flight of steps cut through quartz and gneiss under the dark canopy of the forest. The yaks had started at dawn and were taking a gentler, and longer, route. After a steady climb of about 1,000 feet, fog billowed up from the ravine and closed in. This, and the loose gravel on the steep track, slowed us down. We stopped every few steps, propped our rucksacks against the boulders, and gasped for breath. Beards of moss hung from low rhododendron branches, an astral light seeped through, crows cawed. These were large mountain crows, with thick beaks and bluish black feathers. We had been seeing them since Deoningalo Dhap, sometimes flying in pairs, circling the skies in dizzying displays of grace and wing power. Perhaps they were following us for leftover food.

The march from the dry lake bed of Deoningalo Dhap to Thulo Dhap was the longest. We had to cross a series of connected ridges, continually climbing up and down, through damp shadowy forests of bamboo, oak, rhododendron and other conifers. A number of streams cut the path, with logs laid over them. We were told that the place was named Jorebato, the grove of jori-buti or medicinal herbs. Pasang pointed to some rare herbs that grew on the forest floor where sunlight scarcely entered. They peeped through cracks in the rock and glowed fluorescent green. Here, every square inch of stone or tree trunk was carpeted with green-yellow moss, lichen, wisps of black moss hanging from the low rhododendron branches that was locally known as Old Man's Beard. Rhododendrons are extremely slow-growing plants, Dr. Joshi informed us, and some of the stunted trees with gnarled branches were in fact more than a hundred years old. They did appear like ancient men bent double, with matted body hair on their wiry limbs.

'This is a krummolhz zone,' Joshi said. 'Krummolhz means bent wood. During the long winter, these trees remain weighed down with heavy snow. The deer in the forest quench their thirst by licking the Old Man's Beard.'

Joshi was a senior officer in the Indian Forest Service, currently on deputation in the state tourism department. A tall, thickset man in his early forties, he had got his doctorate in Botany from Delhi University. A fairly long stint in the bureaucracy couldn't kill his love for adventure. So, after the inauguration ceremony of this trek programme, he didn't return to Gangtok after the ritual of speeches and joined us instead.

'Who'd miss the opportunity of a ramble in the forest, that too on duty?' he had told me with a mischievous smile. He stayed alone in Gangtok, his family lived in Lucknow.

And he had been making full use of the opportunity: studying and photographing different species of birds, flowers and insects. During the trek, we'd often find him standing on the edge of a khud, a field-glass trained to a forest of bamboos for the elusive red panda; or else he'd be crouching over a stone for minutes, his camera aimed at a rare butterfly, waiting for it to open its wings. Before this stint, Joshi had been the Divisonal Forest Officer in this particular region for three years. He knew the Singalila sanctuary intimately.

'What made you leave the forest department to work in

tourism?' I asked him. 'Isn't there a conflict of interest between the two?'

My question accentuated the crease on his brow; he tried to offset it with a smile.

'You see, even forest conservation requires funds. A small state like Sikkim has only a few avenues for generating revenue. Tourism is one, the other is hydel power. These are the most happening sectors here,' he said, carefully weighing his words.

From Jorebato, the path wound up to a narrow saddle where three ridges met. A breeze here picked up a steady hum from thick leafless nettles, roused a chorus of cicadas and deepened the solitude of the spot. A type of giant dark mushroom hung like cornices from the stumps of dead trees. A few hundred feet below lay an oval pond, reflecting, like an antique hand mirror, the clouds and rhododendrons in bloom. We now entered a strange charcoal forest.

Two years ago, when Joshi still was the DFO of this division, there had been a big forest fire here. The burnt stumps of the trees had been standing since then. Most were dead, their branches uplifted to the skies like twisted limbs in a final gesture of agony. But a couple of rhododendrons were surprisingly alive, their blackened branches dripping with blood-red blossoms.

'That was the longest night in my life,' Joshi reminisced. 'About twenty of us, forest staff and local villagers included, fought the flames from evening till dawn.'

Nobody had guessed the sweep of the fire. It was the end of winter, the forests were dry as a box of matches. The firefighters scorched off a narrow strip of the jungle to create a barrier against the leaping flames, but it didn't help. The men stood helplessly in a clearing ringed by the parched bed of a seasonal nullah and watched the sparks fly from branch to branch, setting the ancient trees aflame. The dry moss and ferns around the trunks flared up first, like clothes, the flames licking up to the higher branches. Then the upper parts snapped, and finally the thick trunks imploded with a loud bang and cracked open. The blinding blaze and the silhouettes of branches created phantom shadows that appeared like herds of racing deer, leopards and other chimerical beasts. But no animal, not even a bird or a squirrel, was to be found in the forest; they had either fled or perished.

An elemental fear had stunned Joshi and his men on that endless February night. They had sat in a tight circle, some mumbling prayers, waiting for daybreak. The sky was flushed pink from time to time, mimicking sunrise.

We had gathered inside the mess tent at Kalijar for afternoon tea. By then the fog had clotted, daylight had passed into a coma. A wind was blowing over the bare ridge, lashing at the tents with a strange ferocity. But nobody could anticipate that a blizzard would follow so soon. Before it came, there was a sudden drop in temperature. A fire was built with charcoals scavenged from the burnt forest. As we thrust our freezing limbs over the cinders, Dr Joshi narrated to us the incident of forest fire and the longest night in his life. He told us how these fires were caused by careless herdsmen, and how this had forced the forest department to demolish their sheds inside the sanctuary area.

But I failed to find out if the ruins at Kalijar had been herdsmen's sheds or a regular village. The blizzard blew away the mess tent and we had to abandon the plan to climb to Phoktey Dara top.

But the morning turned out clear and dazzling, the spurs and the ridges around were white with fresh snow, and the sky the colour of blue poppies. In the rhododendron grove, upon carpets of snow, there was a massacre of pink and scarlet petals: the young, slanting rays of the sun had set them ablaze. This was the final day of our trek. Now began the downward journey to Chiabhanjan, an outpost on the Indo-Nepal border. But we lost the trail—the stubby concrete markers of the international border had disappeared under the snow—and entered the Border Security Force check post from the Nepal side.

At 5,000 feet, Chiabhanjan was a medley of tin-roofed log cabins, a volleyball court, barbed wire, sandbags, horses, gun muzzles and a limp tricolour atop a flagpole. Only after a thorough check of our identity documents, especially that of the foreigners in our team, were we allowed to step into Indian territory.

The nature of the forest began to change here. There were tall sub-alpine trees whose copper brown leaves were strewn on the stone-lined path. We crossed a number of swift streams, fed by the snow of the previous evening, over logs laid across them. At 4 p.m., we emerged out of the sanctuary and reached Chitrey, a quiet village of Sherpas, our final stop-over. A charming Sherpa-style felicitation ceremony was awaiting us at the head of the village. A group of women dressed in colourful traditional costumes garlanded each participant with faux-silk khadas and offered trays of chhang in pretty little cups and tsamba, roasted buckwheat flour. Custom required of us to put a pinch of tsamba into the cup and drink.

Tashilhunpo Again

At Kangpa-chan, Phurchung's village, the women bade farewell to Sarat Chandra with a chhang-tsamba ceremony. They had gathered at a bridge at the end of the village with stirrup cups, wine and plates full of tsamba. Phurchung's mother was among them. Leaving the village, the party passed a small monastery with a row of Mani wheels being turned by the flowing water of a stream and entered a forest of ancient deodars and silver firs. Sarat and Ugyen were riding ponies. Phurchung marched ahead with the shotgun slung across his back. He had drunk himself blind the evening before, but there was no trace of it in his gait.

On the two visits that Sarat Chandra Das had made to Tibet, Phurchung had been his inseparable shadow, the best companion one could have on such a difficult mission. It was due to him that Sarat gained intimate glimpses of the lives of the mountainfolk on the route. At his village in Kangpa-chan, they had received warm hospitality and gifts—potatoes, butter, millet, beer, and a live lamb. They were also given a stock of blood pudding, sheep's intestine stuffed with a mixture of blood and barley flour, in small cane baskets.

With hired ponies and high-energy food, Sarat and Ugyen had braced themselves for the last and the most difficult stage of their journey—Nango La and Kanglachen. Beyond these passes were the dreaded border guards of the Shigatse province.

The forest was teeming with many species of pheasants and other birds. There were also wild sheep and musk deer here, the coolies said. About 2 miles from the village, they met a group of traders from Yangma with a small train of yak and sheep loaded with blankets, barley, salt and yak hide.

'Is the Kanglachen Pass still open?' Phurchung asked the man with a red head dress and a matchlock rifle on his shoulder, apparently the leader of the group.

'Yes, yes,' he said, clucking his tongue encouragingly. But another man driving the yaks warned that the pass was closed due to heavy snowfall two days earlier.

Beyond a narrow juniper-covered plateau and a steep climb, there was a dry glacier bed. It was ringed by high mountain ranges. Nango La loomed in the distance and, before it, boulders of reddish granite scattered like the ruins of a lost civilization. Dusk had settled when they reached the monastery, the Manding Gompa, which stood on a broad, shrub-covered terrace above a stream. Phurchung arranged lodging for Sarat and Ugyen in a dingy cell inside the gompa. Milk and eggs were procured from the village below. The lamas were busy with their annual dawn-to-dusk reading of sacred sutras; the squat wooden building hummed with their monotonous chants. Two anis, women monks, helped the travellers cook dinner. Meanwhile, Phurchung and his companion Phuntso slipped away for a little revelry in the village.

They didn't return at dinner, or even later at night. After the chanting was over, an eerie silence descended upon the lamasery; it amplified the minutest of noises. Swaddled in blankets inside the dark cold cell, Sarat could hear the murmur of a stream over Ugyen's troubled breath. He could also hear sound of distant music, singing and laughter, faint as a figment of imagination. He remembered the two anis, their round shaved heads and delicate bodies covered in maroon robes. They were silently working a sheep-skin bellows and tending the cooking fire. Their boyish faces glowed in the soot-encrusted darkness. He thought of the village women in this region, their pink, flushed faces, gummy smiles and thick-boned features. A pale moon had broken free of the mountains, it now enamelled the dark forested slopes. He thought of Phurchung and Phuntso carousing in the moonlit village in the company of women. What if they had got drunk and spilled the beans? The thought stung him, and continued to gnaw at his insomnia. That would be the end of the mission, they'd have to turn back. So near, and yet so far—the dashing of a dream! It would mean nothing to these men, just another aborted trip, whose memory would fade before the snow melted on the passes. These men: how they seemed to live from moment to moment, perhaps at that very moment nestled in the warm embrace of a woman. This was a life which Sarat, for all his knowledge, could never fathom.

He didn't know when Phurchung and Phuntso returned. But early in the morning, men from the village, led by the headman, appeared at the gompa's door. The headman was dressed in a flowing robe made of red serge, a Tibetan cap and had long rings on his ears; he came riding a half-breed yak. Sarat introduced themselves as pilgrims.

Why had they chosen such an inappropriate season to go on a pilgrimage? The headman demanded an explanation.

The chaste Tibetan Sarat spoke, lacing it with quotes from sacred texts, and the dress he and Ugyen wore, quelled all misgivings.

'Lhaso! Lhaso!' exclaimed the man on the half-breed yak, and nodded his head. He apologized for not being able to bring any gift.

'Sang poi ja chog!' said Sarat. We'll meet again next year.

'Sang poi ja chog!' the villagers said in a chorus.

But someone from among the crowd pointed a finger and said reproachfully: 'This man is a philing!'

'Yes, he's an Indian!' swore another.

'This Hindu will surely die in the snow!' a third one said. 'His servants will soon return with the news of his death.'

On his first journey two years earlier, Sarat Chandra Das had crossed into Tibet through the Chang-thang La. It was the month of May, there weren't the snow and bitter cold of the November mission. But even so, the path into Tibetan territory was strewn with danger. The valley around the pass was inhabited by Dokpa yak-grazers, a nomadic tribe who were authorized by the Tibetan government to loot and kill trespassers. Sarat had to travel at dusk, hiding behind rocks in the daytime, and crawl across the high arid plateau where every object, every boulder or shrub, was visible for miles around. Danger lurked until he had crossed the river Chorten Nyima and entered Tashilhunpo. There he was greeted by sudden rain, considered a good omen, just after crossing the river. But this time, Sarat and his men were caught in a dust storm in the middle of the dry sandy river bed: clouds of dust and sand tore through the bed like a herd of wild asses and wiped out the view of the surrounding plateau. However, on both the occasions it was a crossing, in the Hindu sense, a pilgrimage, a tirtha.

But before this lay other obstacles, human and natural.

From Manding, the march had continued along the bank of the river Yangma, frozen and empanelled with sheets of ice, in a majestic wilderness of towering mountains. Not a bird in the sky, not a speck of cloud, only the crunch of dry snow under feet in an atmosphere of ghostly silence. The valley gradually widened until they came to the bank of an unfrozen pool. Now the ascent began over a huge glacier, 3 miles long and a quarter of a mile wide. They entered a black-and-white world of bare granite and snow. The night halt had been planned in a permanent cave of ice known as Phugpa-karpo, but darkness overtook them before they could find it. Darkness, dense fog and deadly crevasses at every step. Chilled to the bones, devastated by hunger, thirst and the thin air, they gave up the search for Phugpa-karpo and braced themselves to spend the night under the open sky. Powdery snow blew in through the night, burying them, a dull moon glowed over a zone of death echoing with the rumble of avalanches. It was a most trying night, Sarat would write, never to be forgotten.

The first light of the morning touched everything with fingers of gold, the Kanglachen mountain glowed majestically before their raw eyes. Fortunately, there had been no fresh snowfall at night. The men now laboured up to the crest of the pass to be rewarded with a magnificent view: the sky deep blue, and the unbroken sweep of white crenelated ranges in the north and north-western horizon. Tibet at last!

From here the colour of the mountains began to change: the snow-white on the Indian side graded into blackish grey and ochre brown. After a steady descent down the moraine beds, the warm greens of the treeline and the murmur of streams returned like a reassuring touch. Birds were pecking at juniper berries, yaks were grazing in the valley, ribbons of smoke curled up from the herders' tents. After two days of near starvation, the weary travellers had their fill of steaming rice and butter tea.

It was the 1st of December. Now only one obstacle remained, a human obstacle: the feared guards at Tashi Rabka. To hoodwink them was the most difficult part of the mission.

Tashi Rabka was in the frontier district of Tibet. Years ago, when the Yangma and Wallung districts were part of the kingdom of Sikkim, the king and his retinue would rest here on their way to Shigatse. The ruins of the stage house could be seen on top of a huge boulder. A family of herdsmen had pitched their tents below it. Two dusky women sat there with a fierce-looking mastiff. Phurchung went to greet them, to collect information, and was offered a bowl of tarra, fermented yogurt.

Sarat and his men hid behind rocks near the village, waiting for the cover of darkness. The moon rose late in the evening. Under its spectral light, they could see the stone wall across the slope built during the Gorkha invasion of Tibet earlier in the century. The wall ran up to the edge of the river where it had become a bridge made with stone and logs, with eight watch towers on it. Seeing the fortifications, Phurchung lost his nerve.

Sarat loaded his revolver before they stepped out of the hiding place; Lama Ugyen, too, had armed himself with a Bhutanese knife and a pistol. It was the dead of night: the entire village was sleeping, not a lamp was burning in any of the cottages. The men tiptoed towards the bridge. Phurchung and Ugyen were shaking with fear. A night bird called intermittently, the torrent gurgled under the bridge. Only Phuntso remained calm. He devised a plan: they would sing Wallung walking songs if they found the guards awake and pass themselves off as Wallungpa. With their hearts in their mouths, the men filed past the chortens by the bridge. Everything was clearly outlined under the light of the moon.

'Who are you? Where're you going?' A sleepy voice called out from inside a yak-hair tent.

'We are Wallungpa, going to Shigatse,' replied Phuntso.

Without another word, they crossed the bridge and hurried past the guard commander's post. A chained mastiff was lying curled up on the doorstep under the pale moon-shadow of a watch tower.

All the anxious thoughts sloughed off from Sarat's mind as he finally set foot in Tashilhunpo. Now the memories of his first visit were returning, memories stored away in the folds of dreams, followed by recognition only a fraction of a second after the sightings: of windswept plains and low sandy hills, of kites circling the skies and flocks of swallows like showers of arrowheads, of fields of barley and swarthy women in striking headgear, of rice merchants and their caravan of donkeys. At Tanglung, a village of flat-roofed houses guarded by irregular stone walls, he met Nabu Wanga, an old acquaintance.

'Pundib-la, chyag-feb-nang!' Nabu Wanga exclaimed with open arms. Welcome, honourable Pundit!

Sarat was given the best room in the house, but he couldn't sleep because of excitement. He got up at 3 in the morning and wore a new formal dress that he had kept for this day. It was 9th December; a fine day with a gentle breeze blowing. They set off, at the break of dawn, along a path that was actually the dry bed of an irrigation canal lined with tall grass. Wild rabbits and foxes darted away at the sound of their footsteps. By the time the sun came up, the road was alive with merchants, all headed for Shigatse with loaded caravans of yaks and donkeys.

At noon Sarat came to a quiet tavern on the brow of a hill. He had rested here on his last visit. Nothing had changed. Boulders lay everywhere with the Mani mantra painted on them in red and yellow. There were the tall whispering willows, the big hairy mastiff chained to a post, pigeons cooing on the flat slate roof, and a wizened woman, the innkeeper's mother, sitting on the doorsteps and telling prayer beads. The lines on her face, the fluttering pigeons, the rustle of the willows suggested a still, inviolate rhythm of life that had remained unchanged while the world at large had moved at a feverish pace. Lobden, the innkeeper, came out to greet the Pundit. The mastiff raised its snout and sniffed the air.

They had tea and eggs at the tavern, and when they stepped out, it was late in the afternoon. Steps cut into rocky slopes led down the hill and, rounding a narrow bend, when Sarat looked to the east, his heart skipped a beat.

The river Penam-nyang-chu flowed below the hill, and in the distance rose the snow-capped peaks of the northern Himalaya. In between, across a wide valley, lay Tashilhunpo. The sun was setting in the Indian horizon in an unforgettable display of translucence. It set on fire the golden domes, chortens, spires, palaces and memorials of the monastery town. It was so novel and yet so intimate. Sarat had known this view all along, it seemed, not just from his previous visit, but for a very long time, longer than memory, longer than a lifetime.

George Bogle had described this vision in detail. A hundred years would pass before Sarat Das would set his eyes on it.

Meanwhile, following the Gorkha aggression, Tibet had closed its doors to outsiders. The East India Company's rule had ended, India was part of the British Empire now.

The world, too, had changed. There had been a revolution in France, a new nation had been born in America, and the Industrial Revolution had swept across Europe. The notion of distance and time had been radically altered by steamship and railway, swathes of blank spaces on the world's map been filled up. A year before George Bogle visited Tashilhunpo, a ship's captain named James Cook had set foot on a vast unknown landmass in the western hemisphere, a continent teeming with unknown plants, animals and human tribes. By the time Sarat Chandra would go to Tibet, Australia was a British colony, most of the indigenous population there had been decimated.

But the view of Tashilhunpo from the hill had remained unsullied, constant. George Bogle had recorded his impression in a diary, Sarat Chandra Das was armed with a daguerreotype camera.

WAYS OF SEEING

'The houses of the town rise one above another; four churches with gilt ornaments are mixed with them, and altogether it presents a princely appearance. Many of the courts are spacious, flagged with stone, and with galleries running round them. The alleys, which are likewise paved, are narrow. The palace is appropriated to the Lama and his officers, to temples, granaries, warehouses, &c. The rest of the town is entirely inhabited by priests, who are in number about four thousand. The views of it, which the Lama afterwards gave to me, will convey a better idea of it than any account I can write. For there is no describing a place so as to give others a just notion of it.'

—George Bogle, *Narratives*

'Of yellow skin and short stature, he was wearing an orange brocaded dress. A diamond star glowed on his cap. It seemed as if a celestial being had descended from the mountains around.'

—Alexandra David-Néel, *Magic and Mystery in Tibet*

Kesang Lepcha's Flute

The Tashilhunpo that Sarat Chandra Das had viewed from the top of the hill was imbued with George Bogle's vision. Its description had the rapture of extended time. Twenty years after I read the lines, I visualized the description in a dream. It was like a long pan shot in a movie: innumerable chortens, mendongs, gilt spires and temple domes set ablaze by a brilliant sunset, and, coiling up from it, the simple notes of a flute.

The dream lingered for a length of time, until the spires and domes, columns, terraces, windows, paved squares and paths, and the shadows on them, became distinct. Then it was rent asunder by a rooster's call. I opened my eyes to an unfamiliar room—a small wood-panelled room where daylight streamed in through white lace curtains. The haunting tune on the flute was entwined in the arabesques of light. The rooster's call, the squelch of slippers on wooden floors, the gurgle of water and cows lowing in the distance woke me up fully, but the flute continued. I rubbed my eyes and looked around: a well-appointed room, a pair of cane armchairs, a wardrobe, cotton carpet on the wooden floor, a pair of velvet slippers near the bathroom door and, on the wall, the sepia photograph of a farmer couple. Outside the window, under the eaves, hung rows of yellow corn cobs.

At the end of the trek in Singalila, we had been transferred to a nearby resort. A programme was organized there in the evening on the resort's lawn. A troupe of girls dressed in traditional costumes gave a song-and-dance presentation of rituals related to farming and community life. This was followed by speeches and a vote of thanks. We learnt that the next morning we'd be divided into small groups and taken to homestay facilities for two days and a night. This was part of the package, to let us sample local tribal hospitality and see their life from up close.

After days of togetherness, the farewell hour was touched with a sweet sadness. Dr. Joshi had exchanged his jeans and T-shirt for the bureaucratic suit and was going back to Gangtok. The women's troupe, also from the state capital, were returning with his entourage. In bright daylight, it was impossible to find the farmer women of the previous evening from among the city-slick girls. I had last seen Purba the singer after the evening programme in a corridor behind the dining hall. He was eating. It was dark, the blind man was sitting on his haunches upon the floor and eating slowly from a bowl; a grey dog sat before him with quiet expectancy. I learnt that he had set off at dawn for his village, a day's march away, on foot.

My companion and I, and a French couple, were allocated Tshering Lepcha's homestay in Martam village. Thirty-something Tshering, of athletic build and an ever-ready smile on his face, had come driving his own Scorpio to collect the guests. He gave us a PowerPoint presentation of his homestay facility on the resort's computer, and promised to show us a couple of tourist points on the way to his house.

Tshering Lepcha was a graduate from the government college in Gangtok. Like him, most homestay owners we met were young, educated, tech-savvy and fluent in English. They had an association which helped them get bank loans and training, and also connect to tourists. Around a thousand families in Sikkim were earning their livelihood this way, we were told; no small feat in a state with a population of six lakhs and meagre employment opportunities. But I found something a little disconcerting: there was a covert scramble going on to catch the few Western tourists in the group. Finally, it appeared that they had come up with a solution: they divided us into mixed groups. But this couldn't satisfy them all as the proportion of foreigners to Indians was one to four. My companion and I were allotted Tshering Lepcha's place as appendages to the French couple.

But they were neither fully French, nor a wedded couple. The woman was of South Asian origin, and they were living together; both were in their mid-thirties. They had been travelling in India and Nepal, especially in the Himalaya, with lavish time and a tight budget. They had come to know about this trek programme while they were passing through Gangtok.

Actually, Yann didn't fit into the stereotype of a French man popular in our part of the world: he was neither lanky nor a raconteur. Reticent, hefty and with a shaved head, he looked more German than French. Malee, his girlfriend, was short, springy and with straight black hair; she was affable and ebullient, and was more fluent in English than Yann. During the trek, she used to join us at evening gatherings round the fire or in the mess tent. But they'd always reach the campsite ahead of the others and select the most isolated tent. Possibly Yann wanted it that way. During the blizzard at Kalijar, their tent was the most secured because they had got it pitched between the ruined walls of a hut. Every morning Yann could be seen under a solitary tree or upon a boulder, meditating in the lotus posture.

Tourism and tarmacadam roads seemed to be going hand in

hand in the remotest corners of western Sikkim. Its proximity to international borders helped it get generous funds from the Centre, but the initiative of the local government was remarkable. When I pointed this out, Tshering Lepcha took his right hand off the steering wheel and fished out a USB dongle from his shirt's pocket.

'And this,' he said. 'Mobile signals are now available everywhere. Our business depends heavily on the internet. Bookings and payments are mostly done online.'

And truly, the verdant hills and ridge tops bristled with microwave towers; they were the chortens of the 21st century. Big wayside hoardings pampered the eye with high-definition images of luxury and adventure—from plush hotels and resorts to river cruises upon the Teesta.

Our first stop was at Singshore bridge, the second highest suspension bridge in Asia. In the crowd of tourists flocking at the sagging belly of the bridge, busily squeezing in the towering mountains and the bottomless gorge into the selfie frames, we spotted a few fellow trekkers. After another session of hi-and-byes, we rushed to our next stop, or what is called 'point' in the lingo of hill tourism. It was a giant Mani wheel.

On the outskirts of Hee village, in a deep stream-cut, a huge prayer wheel was being assembled. It had a budget of one crore rupees, Tshering told us, and it would be the largest in the world. From the road, a long flight of steps reached up to the contraption under a concrete pavilion. The water of the spring was being diverted to turn the wheel. Work was going on at full swing inside a makeshift workshop. Workers from North India were giving finishing touches to pieces of moulded fibre with Buddhist symbols and letters on them in relief. Below it, a washroom was being built for the tourists, its drainage being connected to the rechannelled spring at a respectable level below the sacred wheel. Across the gorge, on the sheer cliff, large ferns fluttered like prayer flags, bees were busy building hives under the crags, tiny birds kept up their indomitable orchestra against the roaring spring—all oblivious of the one-crore-rupee 'point' being built. Where would they all go when the place would be crawling with car-loads of tourists? I wondered.

A café had come up in anticipation of that day. Spotting it, Malee became thirsty. 'Ah, tea!' she exclaimed, pronouncing 'tea' in a way that rhymed with 'gay', and barged into the shop with her sunglasses pushed over the brow. And seeing a woman there folding momos, she became hungry too. Tshering ordered momos for us all. All except Yann, who searched for an appropriate snack in the forest of chips, biscuits, chocolates, dried fruits, soft drink and beer cans laid out at the shop's window, and began to study the fine print on them with a scholarly face.

All the packets, tetra packs and cans were made from plastic and aluminium; on each item were printed the price, date of manufacture, ingredients, chemical grades of the colour and preservatives, caloric break-up and the address of the company, which could be anywhere between Surat and Shanghai, Pune and Penang, Ghaziabad and Guangzhou. What was not printed of course was the amount of fossil fuel that had been burnt to transport them to this remote mountain region; for how long these foils and cans would remain undegraded was also not printed.

After visits to the giant prayer wheel at Hee, a crafts museum at Bermiok and a cheese factory at Dentam, we reached Tshering

Lepcha's house late in the afternoon. Fog had dimmed the daylight, and a brief shower had slickened the road. The house stood under a pine grove about a hundred feet from the asphalt road. The tall trees, with raindrops dripping from their branches, cast a darker shadow. The village and its terraced fields fanned out on the slope below.

The front gate of the Tshering House was made from yellow bamboo tied with canes, under an arched trelliswork laden with dark green creepers. It made a pretty picture frame for an old man standing there to welcome us. He was wearing a split-bamboo hat, from which emerged a thin braid of hair and fell on his nape. Everything about his face—the few strands of hair on the chin, the gimlet eyes and lines unfurling from their corners—seemed to contribute to the broad, warm smile on his lips. He took the bags from our hands, despite our protests, and led us into the house along a pebbled walkway.

He was Kesang Lepcha, Tshering's father. We were also introduced to his mother, his wife, an aunt and even their pet dog and cat. His mother and aunt were wearing traditional attire, multi-coloured cotton robes held at the waist with bands; his wife wore kurta and jeans. The dog, a slate-grey Bhotia bitch, was pregnant. The house, with thick walls of stone and mortar and corrugated tin roofs, had a kitchen garden, a poultry shed and a cow shed converted into a garage. Standing at the end of the garden was the double-storeyed cottage made entirely of wood, for the guests. It was picture perfect, literally, the life-size original of the photographs we had seen on the resort's computer. Inside its ground-floor sitting room, Tshering's mother gave us a ceremonial welcome with khadas. She also put marks of rice-flour paste on our foreheads and touched the heads of the two women guests with ripe barley stalks. She was followed by Tshering's aunt who came carrying tea in beautiful porcelain cups and his wife with a tray of fried doughnuts. They all had broad, silent smiles on their lips.

Tshering did all the talking. He reeled out an introduction to his family, his household and his village. I don't know why, but it struck me as a scripted pageant where everyone, even the animals, dutifully played their part: the dog lay on the doormat and the cat leapt into Tshering's lap and watched us like the presiding deity of the house. Only Kesang Lepcha was out of sight; he had slipped into the kitchen garden after depositing our bags in the bedrooms upstairs. All the vegetables on their dinner table came from the garden, Tshering announced affectedly: 'Hundred per cent organic farming!'

The sitting-room of the guest cottage was furnished with care. The seating arrangement was on the wooden floor, upon rugs and thick cushions, with low painted tables usually seen in Buddhist temples. There were heavy stone grinders, drums, spears and other traditional bric-a-brac arrayed in the corners. On the walls were framed family photographs, recently taken but tinted sepia, a row of peaked leather caps adorned with feathers, a big colour blow-up of Chief Minister Pawan Chamling and a large LCD television set. Except the last two, each item in the room appeared to be strung together by the silent narrative of a museum. A living museum.

Was it part of the protocol set by the home-stay organization? I never got around to asking Tshering. But from the moment we stepped into their house, I had this queasy feeling. Sitting in the wide dining area attached to the kitchen, in our attempts at table talk across the hurdle of languages, or during the gentle jokes Tshering cracked about members of the household, the feeling never left me. It seemed that a way of life, as complex and ordinary as it is everywhere in the world, was being unfurled before the visitors' eyes in an attractive, decipherable format.

We were to leave the next morning. Had we stayed back, the things we could do, the places around the village we could visit, the short rambling treks we could undertake—'activities', as Tshering said—had all been preset. Perhaps the harried, city-pent tourist wanted it that way, a package where the ethnic would seamlessly blend with the functional: a traditional welcoming ritual with a modern bathroom, the sense of the remote and the exotic with smooth mobile telecommunication. There was nothing wrong in this. But after spending four days out in the middle of open, unalloyed nature, the small details stood out rather sharply.

Life in the mountains was changing; the people, nature, even the skylines were changing. The springs were clogged with plastic, the air in the village square thick with diesel fumes and rancour. The images of life that George Bogle had seen, that Sarat Das had seen, that had remained constant for two hundred years, were fading, had faded away irretrievably. These thoughts lurked in my subconscious mind on the morning I had the dream of Tashilhunpo as Sarat Das, and before him George Bogle, had seen: the roofs and spires of countless chortens, gompas and temples gleaming in the sun, and rising from it the sad haunting tune of a flute.

A rooster's call ripped open the dream, but the flute continued. Kesang Lepcha was playing it.

In a corner of the garden of Tshering House, behind a plot of maize, was a tiny prayer room made of stone and shaped like a gazebo. Kesang Lepcha would go there every morning before sunrise. Inside the low bare room was a yak-hair rug on the floor and a low desk, on which sat a leather-bound book and a large bamboo flute. Kesang would sit on the rug and read aloud from the book, invoking Mother Earth, asking for her blessings and forgiveness before he entered into her world on another new day. Then he would pick up the flute and blow a simple tune into it, calling on the newborn day of the telluric world, its trees, creepers, birds, stones, worms, springs and the spirits who inhabited them.

Kesang Lepcha was an animist, an adherent of the ancient Bon faith that had been popular in these regions many centuries ago. Eleven families in the village still followed this faith, though they were enlisted in census records as Buddhist. They also observed all the major rituals in the Buddhist calendar.

We learnt all this during morning tea in the old house. On his way back from the prayer room, Kesang had picked green raspberries for us. Unripe and tangy, their taste combined well with the yellow Gouda cheese we had bought the day before from the cheese factory at Dentam. The name of the cheese had come from the town of Gouda in Netherlands, Yann informed us, the town famous for cheese making. We also learnt that a type of grass growing in high Alpine meadows gave the cheese its distinctive flavour.

Yann's reserve had slipped away on the bright crisp morning; he was in a chatty mood. Malee was yet to be up and about.

The kitchen opened out to the dining area, spacious and airy, with old flagstones on the floor. There was a traditional clay oven, with faggots neatly stacked on a loft, and also a gas range. One wall was taken up by a cabinet crammed with crockeries, glassware and various household gadgets, including a microwave oven. Strings of maize, garlic and dried mushrooms hung from the rafters, and on rough wooden shelves were arrayed bottles of pickled bamboo shoots, cherry peppers, tree tomatoes and other local vegetables. A narrow porch led to the garden, where a profusion of pale green squash fruits hung from a bamboo trellis. Under it, on sun-dappled grass, the cat was distractedly chasing a pair of silvery butterflies. The dog was curled up as usual on the doormat.

Tshering was helping his wife prepare breakfast for us. His mother, a blue handkerchief tied around her head and her feet shod in plastic gumboots, was cleaning out the poultry shed in the garden. Radio Nepal was playing on a sideboard. The everyday picture of an ordinary household, unscripted and unbidden.

Kesang carried live cinders in a cast iron pan and placed it near our feet. He sat before us on a low stool and began to speak about the land of his origin.

'You hear Dzongu? I am from Dzongu,' he said, patting his chest, and then pointed to his wife in the garden. 'And she, and my sister.'

'Not he?' Yann asked, pointing to Tshering.

'No, not he,' Kesang said, and then quickly corrected himself with a toothy smile. 'Yes he, and she, and everyone. All we Rong Lepcha people from Dzongu. We come from there, we go there when die. So he, yes. But not from my village in Dzongu. He born here, Martam. From Dzongu village, only me, my wife, my sister. We grow cardamom in village, not now. But we all come from there, we all go there. To Dzongu. But they make big dam in valley. So where we go from here?'

A deep anxiety rang in his voice and accentuated the lines on his face.

The Lepchas have always considered the Dzongu Valley as their sacred homeland. It was believed that the tribe originated there during the dawn of creation and, even now, when a member died, the soul left the corporeal body and returned to the valley. The Dzongu Valley had been declared a protected sanctuary. But here, as elsewhere, development had cast its long shadow.

'A number of big hydel power projects are being constructed on the Teesta river,' I told Yann, trying to clue him into Kesang Lepcha's narrative.

'Altogether twenty-six,' Tshering said. 'The largest of them is being built right on the headwaters of Teesta. We are protesting this.'

Before joining the trek programme, Yann and Malee had been to Yumthang Valley; they had seen the construction work on the way. Yann described how surreal the massive concrete dykes and buttresses appeared on the pristine mountainside.

Kesang Lepcha narrated excitedly, gesturing with his hands, how the forests and the mountain had been ravaged by these projects. Not only had trees been cut and the forests laid waste, but the ethnic character of the place had changed because of the influx of outsiders on works related to dam construction.

As I listened to them, I meditated on the idea of an imagined land imbued with a certain aura of faith, to which generations of men like Kesang Lepcha yearned to return after death, a land he invoked every day by blowing into a bamboo flute. I remembered a British woman named Julia Griffith who had come to Darjeeling many years ago to study the culture and rituals of the Lepcha tribe, particularly the pre-Buddhist animist practices. Truth be told, she couldn't find anything substantial. And here I found Kesang Lepcha.

After breakfast, my companion and I were to set off for Rinchenpong. Yann and Malee were to visit Phodong monastery on their way to Gangtok, where they planned to stay a few days before heading south. As we took leave of the family and hit the road, memories of Julia Griffith rushed back to my mind. I had hung out with her during the few weeks she had stayed in Darjeeling and had accompanied her on some of her field trips. I was then a newcomer to Darjeeling, still wearing the blinkers of middle-class Bengali romanticism about the hill town. After I met her, I began to see the British-built hill station from a new perspective, and learnt to detect the mists of nostalgia that overlaid it.

And I had continued to seek these perspectives. Even on the trek through the Singalila forest. I had tried to see, through the writings of an English botanist and a Bengali schoolmaster, the mountains, the trees, the birds, the stones and even the remains of a lost village. But I had completely forgotten Julia Griffith. Her memories unspooled back to me now like the strains of the flute I had heard at dawn.

A bustling market had come up around the taxi stand in Rinchenpong; the tide of tourism had swelled in what had been, even a few years ago, a sleepy wayside village. New hotels and lodges had reared their concrete-and-glass heads on the green hillside. What had remained unchanged were the old, raisin-skinned women who sat in the market square with wild fruits, herbs and mushrooms, their quaint costumes and slit-eyed smiles. And of course the inviolable mountains. A sweep of the great ranges was visible from here, including the peaks of Kabru, Pandim, Kumbhakarna and other neighbours of Kanchenjunga.

From the taxi stand, flights of steps climbed up to the top of the hill, alongside vegetable gardens and homestead lands, to taper into a foot track through a grove of old cryptomeria pines. The din of the market fell away like a withered leaf as we entered it. Now we could hear birdsong and see the distant snow-covered mountains through the dark filigree of leaves. But by the time we climbed up to the monastery on the flat top of the hill, fog had billowed up from the valley to shut off the view.

The ancient gompa, made of wood and blocks of stone, sat on a wide clearing. Lama Ugyen Gyatso had received training here one hundred and fifty years ago. Now we saw a bunch of little lamas chasing each other on the grass, their maroon robes flapping against the fog amid shouts and laughter.

Suddenly I heard someone call, 'Ugyen! Chhitto! Chhitto!'

A boy leapt out of the fog and stopped inches before me. He was panting heavily. His startled eyes were clear as glass and a blue vein ran across his shaved skull like a thread.

On one side of the flat ground, on a rise, stood a blur of birches and magnolias. A breeze was blowing over their crowns. Countless silken prayer flags tied on bamboo poles lashed the luminous greyness with the sound of beating hearts.

In 1912, a European woman had come to this region, drawn by Buddhism and Eastern mysticism. Her name was Alexandra David-Néel. In the kingdom of Sikkim, she had met the crown prince Sidkeong Tulku Namgyal. The prince was a reincarnated lama, but he also had an Oxford degree. He and Alexandra became great friends, perhaps fell in love with each other. They had met here in this monastery, on this very ground, in this heart-thumping forest of prayer flags. Tulku was thirty-two then, Alexandra over forty. He would die four years later. Alexandra David-Néel would live on till she was one hundred and two. She would remember their first meeting until the last day of her life. The prince, in an orange brocaded dress and a diamond gleaming on his cap, was riding a horse. Behind him stood his retinue of men, dressed in the colours of the rainbow. It scarcely seemed he was a person of flesh and blood. Alexandra didn't dare close her eyes, for she feared the spectacle would vanish like a dream.

We walked down the avenue of flags and entered the dark temple hall. A recital of sutras had just ended and a thin young lama was rolling up the long narrow rugs. A butter lamp burned on the altar. In its weak light a dark-skinned Buddha appeared to be suspended in richly painted darkness. He sat cross-legged in the posture of meditation, but his eyes were opened wide in an expression of startled amazement. A naked white woman sat astride him on his lap, facing him, her arms and legs tied around his body in a tight embrace.

The Blue Serpent

Kinthup's first glimpse of the Dihang as it leapt into the plains of Assam was filled with an indescribable excitement. The same feeling struck him again when he saw, after four years, the town of Darjeeling from a hilltop across the Rangeet. He had to turn back from the Assam frontier because the war-like Abors lived in the region. It had taken him another five months to reach here.

It was late in the afternoon, the sun had dipped behind the mountains. A grey nimbus hung low over the distant sanatorium, accentuating the tiny white buildings on the brow of the spur. Kinthup had found shelter in a herdsman's dwelling. In the evening, the cloud over Darjeeling wasted away and the lights of the town twinkled feebly, like glow worms in the boundless darkness.

After the four punishing years of exile, how did Kinthup feel on seeing the lights? In the twinkling cluster, did he search for a lone speck of light burning in Butcher Bustee? There is no way of knowing; naturally, such thoughts were not included in the report that had been prepared after his return.

But on that night his mind was filled with a quiet glow of satisfaction; he couldn't sleep for the excitement. In the herdsman's cottage, he was given a pallet in a low dung-plastered cellar, amid ears of corn and farm implements. Through chinks in the wooden roof, sounds of domesticity seeped in late into the night: the tinkle of pots, the bawl of a baby, the drowsy buzz of a man and a woman talking. Next day, Kinthup left before dawn.

It was a bright sunny morning by the time he came to the riverbank. Rangeet flowed swiftly, unfurling plumes of spray against the smooth boulders. A cane bridge spanned it. A cluster of Limbu huts stood on the other side, and long conical cane fishing nets propped against the walls. Kinthup took the path that wound up through a forest of plantain, passed a row of thatched sheds where two Mech coolies were sleeping on a heap of potatoes. The sheds hadn't been there before. Further up, he met a group of Tibetan traders leading mules with huge loads on them. The nearer he approached Darjeeling, the stranger it all appeared. The forested slopes below the sanatorium had given way to swathes of young tea plants, clusters of white cottages with green tin roofs peeped out from the foliage above. A suspicion rose in Kinthup's mind: had he lost his way? Was he heading to an unknown town? But how could he ever mistake the contours of the ridge, the curve of the river down below? He continued to push on and met a pair of woodcutters coming down the path. They confirmed: yes, this *was* Darjeeling.

But when Kinthup finally made to the tail of the Cart Road on the narrow tip of the spur, near the village of Alebong, he lost his bearings. This surely wasn't the town he had departed from. On that crisp, sunny day, numberless bullock carts were rattling down the road, strangely dressed people milled about, new buildings stood everywhere. The market square was buzzing like a fairground. After all these years spent in the most desolate of terrains, Kinthup's mind was completely boggled at seeing so many people together in one place. He drifted through the crowd like a sleepwalker. Seeing his ragged dress and the stupefied look on his face, a mendicant monk shouted a curse, a pair of Gorkha girls sporting silk stockings and pumps laughed, patted their lips and cried out—'Ammammamma!'

Now, as he left the bazaar and advanced further into the town, he failed to understand the language people spoke on the street. He passed a row of butchers' stalls, timber sheds, a jhampani depot, and when he came near a bend in the road, he heard a strange metallic noise. It began to grow rapidly, and advanced from around the bend. A landslip had occurred nearby, it seemed, and countless boulders were rolling down. No, not boulders of stone, but of metal, hitting against each other and clanging down the hillside. But surprisingly, the people on the street were completely at ease and going about their business. To Kinthup, it all appeared like a dream.

And then he saw it. Not a dream, but a nightmare that had watched over his insomnia night after night from a wall in the Marpung lamasery: a bizarre blue serpent. By some miracle, it had come down on the town's road in broad daylight and was slithering forward at an incredible speed, hissing with rage and belching smoke from its head. It had gobbled up dozens of sahib-mems who were peeping out from inside its belly.

'Naag! Naag!' Kinthup shouted in terror, turned back and began to run. The steel beast of his nightmare chased him, emitting sharp, blood-curdling grunts. People stopped on the wayside to watch the fun, the Madhesi cart drivers tsk-tsked their tongues, the jhampani boys hooted, and yet Kinthup ran for his dear life.

An Englishman on a horse was cantering down the road from the opposite direction; Kinthup slammed into him. Scarcely had the sahib grabbed his hair and pulled him off the steel tracks on to the road than Kinthup hugged his riding boot and wailed: 'Naag! Sahib, naag!'

The Englishman, of deep blue eyes and muttonchop sideburns, shook the poor man by his shoulder and shouted through the deafening roar of pistons, levers and the wheels, 'It's a train, you bloody fool! A train!'

Four years ago, when Kinthup left Darjeeling, a railway track was being laid alongside the Cart Road. The jungle below the St. Columba's Church had been cleared and cuttings made on the slopes; prefabricated pieces of viaducts were being carried up on bullock carts from Siliguri all through the day. A number of men and women from his bustee, too, had been drafted into the coolie gang. But Kinthup had never seen a train before, he never knew how this marvellous steel beast had changed the quiet hill town.

A Pair of Eyes

There was a time when Darjeeling was the gateway to Tibet. Scholars, spies, invaders, mystics and plant hunters flocked to this town before making forays into the forbidden land. The goods of an industrial civilization were sent there through the market here. Tibetan traders, too, used to come with their mule trains when the snow melted over the passes. But when I went to work there in the 1990s, it was impossible to imagine that this crowded tourist town had once been the frontier outpost of a great empire, wedged between two independent kingdoms, and looked out to a third, a land of mystery and magic. That geopolitical perspective had slipped off long ago: Sikkim was now a part of India and Tibet a part of China. Darjeeling was now just another hill town, a lump in the mountain studded with touristy 'points', just a point really, a centre whose circumference had been erased.

One of those years I didn't return home to Kolkata during the long winter vacation in college. After my colleagues had trooped back to the plains and the students had vacated the hostels, the campus became completely deserted. Jackals roamed around the locked staff quarters after dark. Lights could still be seen in a couple of the bungalows, as in Dr. Norbu's, but I didn't have the heart to meet the people I knew. With every passing day, the winter cold tightened its grip like a vice, the familiar faces on the streets and the bazaar became scarce.

Drifting about like a stranger in a familiar town, I discovered a new taste of freedom.

Christmas came and the shops at Chowrasta and the Gymkhana Club decked up for the occasion. But all the glitter and laughter, the strains of guitars in pubs and the deep organ music in St. Andrew's Church never reached down to the bazaar area. The town split into two along the Cart Road, as it had always been during the British times: the and its surroundings being the exclusive domain of sahib-mems, and the natives huddled around the Chowkbazaar and below. As the temperature dropped further, the population thinned there. Most of the shops folded. I roamed the lanes of the bazaar and watched flocks of pigeons on the empty square, under a pallid sun, and knots of porters huddled around burning trash. The Chowkbazaar would turn empty before the daylight faded, the last-turn service taxis having left early.

One day, as I was walking past the desolate taxi stand in the gathering dusk, a thin voice called out: 'Daju, ekchhin!'

I turned to find a man in a threadbare coat and pyjamas. A few feet away from him stood a young woman; she was wearing a ghagra-choli and a thin blue scarf draped around her shoulders. Seeing me stop, the man shuffled forward and began to narrate his story in a low, tired voice; the woman stood where she was. They had come to town by the morning bus from Bijanbari, a distant village, to see a doctor at the Sadar hospital. But it had taken them the entire day because of the long queue at the Out Patients' Department. Meanwhile, the last bus to Bijanbari had left. The money they had with them was spent in buying medicines, and there wasn't enough left to take a room in a hotel. They didn't know what to do, where to spend the long, freezing night.

The despondency in the man's voice touched me. I gave him some money, enough to rent a room in a cheap lodge for the night. But it seemed to me that he was disconcerted by my gesture. He took the money hesitantly and said rather coldly, 'Shukriya.'

Just at that moment a car with its headlights on sped past us, the face of the woman shone for a brief instant: she had a pair of large kohl-lined eyes set in a dark oval face with a gleaming nose stud on it. Not a hill woman.

I had forgotten the incident. Many weeks later, at exactly the same spot and the same hour of the dusk—by then the temperature had dropped further and the streets were almost empty—I heard the call again: 'Ekchhin, daju!'

I was wearing a woollen cap, but when I turned to look, he immediately recognized me and didn't come forward. The woman was standing against the railing, dressed in the same ghagra-choli, the same blue scarf now covering her head like a veil. The man sidled away, but the woman stood where she was, staring at me.

I returned to my icy apartment with a cloud inside my head. Was the man her father, her husband, or...someone else? Were they Madhesi, from the plains? I recalled her face I had seen for an instant, lit up by the headlights of a passing car. It seemed I had known that face and those large animal eyes.

It was in Pablo Neruda's *Memoirs*. During his solitary days in Ceylon as a consul, the young poet used to live in a secluded log cabin on the outskirts of Colombo. It had a primitive lavatory in the garden, which a Tamil woman of the pariah caste would clean every morning. Dressed in a cheap red saree, heavy glass bangles on her arms and ankles, and a red glass nose stud that sparkled like a ruby, she was the most beautiful woman Neruda had seen in Ceylon. She walked like an indifferent goddess, with the pail of excrement balanced on her head, and returned back to the mysterious forest. The poet was smitten with her. He kept little presents on her path to seduce her, but the woman remained completely indifferent, like a wild animal. As the intriguing ritual went on morning after morning, young Neruda couldn't take it anymore.

One day, he grabbed her by the wrist and pulled her to his camp bed. She didn't resist, neither did she respond. As the poet tugged away the flimsy saree to uncover the fabulously sculpted figure he had seen on the temple walls of Asia, she surrendered herself with a stony silence, fixing her cold animal eyes on him.

That image, those large animal eyes, pinned my memories and began to pervade my solitude.

LINES OF FATE

'He pressed me to examine his palm, and stretched it out toward me. How could I refuse, and how could I predict falsely? So I told him that there are certain figures and lines in the palm of the hand from which experts in palmistry can draw indications of a long or short life.'

—Sarat Chandra Das, *Journey to Lhasa and Central Tibet*

'The old man's chains had been removed from his limbs that morning for the first time in twenty years and he came in blinking at the unaccustomed light like a blind man miraculously restored to sight.'

—Edmund Candler, *The Unveiling of Lhasa*

Rinpoche

At Khangsar, in the residence of a wealthy landlord, Sarat Chandra Das met a woman named Rinpoche. During his stay in Tibet as the guest of Panchen Lama's prime minister, he had met many people, both men and women. But he had always referred to them in his books by their title and rank. Rinpoche, the daughter-in-law of his host at Khangsar, the wife of his two sons, was an exception.

Rinpoche was a young lady of about twenty—Sarat had noted in his diary—of modest manners and intelligent looks. She was looking after the guests and lingered until the servants had left.

Ugyen Gyatso started the conversation; he wanted to know her lineage.

'Have you heard the name Kusho Mankipa?' Rinpoche asked him.

'Yes, if you are speaking of Manki, the maternal uncle of the Rajah of Sikkim.'

'That's him,' she replied. 'He was my father. He left for the heavenly abode last year. But such is my misfortune, I couldn't be by his side during his final hour.'

She paused, took a deep breath and continued: 'Are you then the subject of my cousin brother Denjong Gyalpo?'

Ugyen nodded his head in agreement.

'It's been such a long time since I last saw my aunt. I have been married for three years and not once during this time did I visit my country.'

Rinpoche's eyes sparkled, she stood there for a few seconds with lowered head and left the room. Sarat and Ugyen exchanged glances.

But they couldn't meet her husbands; they were away at Shigatse on official business. The family had farms all over the province, also investments in the metal trade. Signs of wealth were visible in their beautifully built house of thick rubble walls and richly carved poplar beams.

Dinner was set in a large hall with a skylight on the roof and thick cushions covered with Khamba carpets laid on the floor. Food was served in Chinese style, on copper plates with chopsticks and spoons. The first course consisted of ribbon-like egg noodles, cooked with minced mutton, with the accompaniment of a soup. Rice and six varieties of meat curry were served next, along with pickled vegetables, black and white mushrooms, a side dish made with a type of Chinese grass, vermicelli, green pea shoots and potato curry. Sweet pilav came on the third, and the fourth course had boiled mutton and tsamba. The repast was rounded off with tea.

The dinner continued for a long time, in absolute silence, with a bevy of servants laying out the dishes one after the other. Ugyen whispered to Sarat that on very special occasions as many as thirteen courses were served in wealthy Tibetan households.

After dinner, they were taken to another room where Angla, the venerable mother of the host, was waiting to receive the guests from India. On a wall were a row of Tibetan masks covered with black cloth and standing in the centre of the room was a jalang, a large bell metal stove with live charcoal in it. Angla's ancient face was set in a mass of pure white hair; it shimmered in the glow of cinders like a herdsman's hut in snow. She raised a withered arm and invited Sarat to sit close to the brazier, upon a pile of cushions. The host and his wife sat by her side. Rinpoche sat behind them with folded knees.

Sarat had learnt Tibetan well, but he needed Ugyen's help to understand the dialect of the old lady.

'In sacred books we've read about the pundits of Aryabarta,' Angla spoke slowly, in a rasping voice. 'They had travelled to remote corners of the earth to spread the word of our Lord. It is our great fortune to have one of them in our house.'

Sarat was surprised by the lively voice that issued out of the gaunt old body. 'In fact it is I who am the fortunate one,' he replied. 'It is by divine grace that we have overcome great obstacles and set foot on this blessed land.'

The conversation veered to the difficult journey they had undertaken, especially at this time of the year, with winter setting in and the passes covered with snow. The host congratulated Sarat and Ugyen for their feat. Now Angla wanted to know about the great Indian cities of Vajrasena, Varanasi and Kapilavastu, of whose glory she had been hearing since childhood, and about Buddhism in modern India.

In a few words, Sarat sketched the state of Buddhism and its practices in India. The country was being ruled by the British, he said, and recently their queen had taken charge from the East India Company. Before them, the Mughals had ruled India for more than two hundred years.

Angla grieved when she learned about the desecration of Buddhist temples and monuments at the hands of zealots. The deep lines fanning out of the corners of her eyes glistened. The atmosphere in the room was turning heavy. The host brought up another topic.

'I know the pundits of India can read the future in the lines on the palm,' he said with a smile. 'Since we have you here, I'd beseech you to read our future.'

Sarat was in a quandary. An English-educated young man with a degree in civil engineering, neither did he have any knowledge of palmistry nor any faith in it. But in George Bogle's diary he had read about the great passion Tibetans had for this occult branch of knowledge. He didn't have the heart to let down his host; moreover, it could make them suspicious about his identity. He thought for a moment and replied:

'Although I have some knowledge of this art, I've doubts whether the lines on the palm can really help foretell a person's future,' he said. 'And, in any case, there's nothing worse than knowing beforehand the miseries that'd befall in course of time. Human life is full of suffering, our Lord had sought nirvana to be freed from them.'

His words, and the way he delivered them, impressed his listeners. But the host persisted; he thrust out his palm and pleaded:

'If only you'd take a look at my life line. I can at least arrange appropriate ceremonies to avert an unnatural cause of death, if there's any.'

How could I refuse, and how could I predict falsely? Sarat thought.

'It's clear as day that your lifeline is quite long, and as to your wealth and fortune … well, everyone knows that god has been kind to you.'

On the timeless image of India cherished by an old Tibetan lady, Sarat Chandra had etched sharp linocuts of decay and ruin.

It was the last quarter of the 19th century. For some time, the wonderful remains of a forgotten past were leaping out from the depths of forests and mounds in different corners of the subcontinent. Earlier in the century, chasing a tiger into a narrow gorge in the lush Deccan plateau, a sahib officer had discovered the painted caves of Ajanta. A few years later, an engineer riding a palanquin in a dense forest in central India had become curious about an ancient temple complex lost in the wilderness. This was the Khajuraho. At that time, a young architect was meticulously sketching the ruins of a huge sun temple on the Orissa coast, known as Konark, that for centuries had helped sailors navigate the choppy waters of the Bay of Bengal. The British political agent at Bhopal made drillings into mysterious spherical stupas at Sanchi in search of hidden treasures. Innumerable major and minor memorials, decayed and smothered by tropical vegetation, were being sighted and unearthed during the great trigonometric survey that had begun in 1802 and continued through the century. A gargantuan archive of data, maps, sketches, lithographs, aquatints, photographs and other materials were piling up in various places, especially in the Asiatic Society in Calcutta.

As an English-educated young man, Sarat Chandra Das was familiar with the idea of a break in the history of this ancient land, a fissure covered over with the detritus of time. In ancient cities like Benaras, layers of time were superimposed, as in a palimpsest. From the *Oriental Scenery* of the Daniells (Thomas Daniell and his nephew, William) in the 18th century to drawings and watercolours by amateur civilians and their memsahibs, countless artworks focussed on this break in history. They depicted fabulous architectural ruins slowly crumbling to dust upon the vast flat plains under a tropical sun, with diminutive natives lounging around them, or going about their humdrum businesses of life: the rich colours of the past washed over by a flimsy mirage of the present.

Sarat's clandestine journey to Tibet was, for him, a search for India's incorruptible past. He wanted to lay his hands on its signs preserved in books and manuscripts in the dry cold climate there, in monastery libraries and private collections, in the womb of an ahistorical time. He went in search of a lost time. The people of Tibet had, on the other hand, received him as a pilgrim from the timeless land, the eternal spring of faith.

But never for a moment did he forget his mission as a spy of the British imperial government. He had made meticulous topographic measurements of all the paths he had traversed and studied the people and their habitats in vivid colours. Living through an experience and, at the same time, putting it on paper, often as a clandestine and risky act, putting himself as a character in the narrative, impersonal but not detached, required of him a rigour of perception, a Western positivist attitude. The people who hosted him in Tibet, on the other hand, had a completely different sense of time and place.

Perhaps such a sense of time and place was still alive in the heart of Kesang Lepcha. The timeless India that the venerable Angla had wished to view through Sarat Chandra, and was heartbroken to learn about its ruin, had a parallel in Kesang's vision of the Dzongu Valley, the homeland of his tribe and the spirit of his ancestors, the source of all the unique forms of life that a hydel project was about to destroy.

But Kesang didn't say these thing in as many words. In fact, we rarely saw him during the two days we stayed in their place. He lurked on the margins of the neat image of a charming Lepcha household that Tshering had laid out before us. Whenever we'd run into him in the garden or in the dining area, he would bow and offer a shy smile. During a light drizzle after dinner, he walked us along the garden path from the main house to the guest cottage holding a large shepherd's umbrella over our heads. He remained practically silent when Tshering was speaking about the protest movements. But on that memorable morning, the music of his flute had expressed more than what words could convey.

The house fell silent at night. A steady wind roared across the vast bare plains outside. The upstairs dormitory assigned to Sarat had parchment window panes with tiny pieces of glass fitted into them. There was a moon in the sky, its dull light radiated through the parchments. Together with the glow from the brazier and a single butter lamp in an alcove, it wove a rare ambience. A pebbled courtyard was visible below through the glass, the smooth stones shone under the moon. A large greyhound, a rarity in this region, was sleeping there. The entire household had gone to sleep, it seemed. A lone lamp burned in a chamber at the end of the screened balcony. Its light cast shadows of intricate latticework on parchment, giving the room the look of a paper lantern.

Sarat was startled by the rustle of silk on the wooden floor. It was Rinpoche; she was carrying a cup of tea.

Of the many don'ts he'd been told before this journey, the most important was never to drink water here. Tibetans normally drank tea to quench their thirst, those who couldn't afford it drank cold chhang instead.

'Hope I'm not disturbing the Pundit's repose,' Rinpoche said.

'Not at all,' Sarat replied. 'In fact I was watching the beautiful moonlight.'

'Yes, today is the thirteenth night of the waxing moon. The sky, too, is clear. But I have come with a request.'

Sarat looked at her. She had changed her evening dress and was now wearing a white silk robe brocaded with silver. Her hair was unbound, the gold ornaments on her arms and neck shone through the silk fabric. She looked ethereal.

'I want you to read my fortune,' Rinpoche said.

Sarat smiled. 'It needs no reading to tell that the great almighty has been very kind to you. But why are you so keen to know your future, Rinpoche?'

'Ah, Rinpoche!' she uttered the word with a sigh. 'This name was given me by my mother-in-law. I had a different name in my father's house.'

Sarat thought of asking it; instead, he said, 'Rinpoche, priceless gem. What an apt name for a handsome and accomplished woman. Your mother-in-law has vision. Your father-in-law, too, is a blessed man. You have two bright husbands, this fine house, such wealth, and I hope you'll soon be a mother.'

Rinpoche stepped forward and kneeled before him on the bare floor. She spoke hurriedly, 'My in-laws are rich, but they work like farmers. I have to slave away from dawn to dusk and obey my mother-in-law's orders—weaving carpets, directing the servants, overseeing cooking. She's a heartless woman. I cannot step out of the house. Even if I do, there's nothing to see—only the endless rocky plains lashed by a bitter wind. It chaps my skin and brings out blood. My home is not like this, there the women don't work so hard. It's in a faraway country, d'you know?'

'Yes, I know,' Sarat replied. 'You are from the royal family of Sikkim.'

'It's in Chumbi Valley. The climate is gentle there, and the land is full of life. It's been three years since I have last seen a green valley, or tasted the sweet rice that grows there.'

Rinpoche paused, and then, raising her face, said in an imploring voice: 'Will you take me there when you return?'

What could he have said? Before him was a woman; an exile living far away from her own people in a cold, rough land, yearning for home.

'Aren't your husbands fond of you?' Sarat asked.

'They remain away from home on business most of the time,' she replied.

Sarat felt a strange dryness in his throat. Rinpoche extended her right hand upon her knee and opened the palm, as if to show him a hidden treasure.

Sarat saw the bare ivory arm coming out of the folds of silk, the open palm and fingers translucent as mother of pearl. It was mesmerizing.

'D'you know where these fine brocaded silks are made?' he managed to say.

Rinpoche smiled sadly. She said: 'My body is made of iron, so thinks my mother-in-law.'

Her eyes were fixed upon Sarat's face, her torso delicately twisted in a gesture of supplication. The moonlight seeping into the room had built up. It appeared as if Rinpoche was made of that light, the robe she wore was a diaphanous mist. The glimmer of cinders caught the hints of a gilded monastery town behind the mist.

'Varanasi!' Sarat said in a thick voice.

He, too, kneeled on the floor, facing Rinpoche, and took her open palm into his. It was soft as feather, and warm. His own hand was damp with an icy sweat.

The Fallout

When I was a child, and had begun to read storybooks on my own, a thought would sometimes cross my mind: when a closed book sat still in the shelf, did the printed letters on the pages also remain quiet? Or did they come alive, change places and go on weaving their own unimaginable stories? A few times I had tiptoed to my father's bookshelf, pulled out a book and opened it to find out. But each time the errant letters would return to their assigned places a fraction of a second before I touched the book, like merry school children in a class at the sound of the teacher's footsteps. I had never been able to catch them playing; though I had seen them glowing with recent exertion. Naturally, I had never shared these thoughts with anyone. It was the period in life when even the most inanimate of objects seemed to have a secret life of their own, that shadowy phase which every boy and girl lives in his and her own way. It is also the time when one emerges from the world of oral tales told by adults, and steps into the world of printed stories. The fluidity of the live telling of tales still remains fresh in the mind.

A residue of such puerile imagination would lurk somewhere in the depths of the mind, to resurface at rare moments: in an intermediate phase between sleep and waking, in the middle of the night, stretched out on a bed and reading a book propped up against the chest, on that very moment before the book would slip off the hands, when the heavy-lidded eyes would open and close like slow moth-wings on a lighted glass pane, and the chest would heave to a gentler rhythm. It is then that the printed letters would begin to dance, change places, peel out of paper and weave marvellous arrangements. Then prismatic dots would appear behind the closed eyelids, like showers of dust from the flapping moth-wings, the moonlight would cast blue filaments crackling on the coat of a sleeping greyhound, pearls of sweat would break out on bared ivory skin, a night bird would call out somewhere on the windy plains, the dog would scratch the paving stones in sleep, the heart would thump against the chest, growing ever louder, until it'd become knocks on the door.

I opened my eyes to see the morning light glistening on the mist streaming down the windowpane, the table lamp still on, and a copy of *Journey to Lhasa and Central Tibet* lying open on the floor. The knocking continued.

Outside the door stood Professor Norbu, his hat and overcoat dusted with pale blue willow blossoms. He had milk packets and a rolled-up newspaper in his hand.

'Good morning! Hope I didn't disturb your sleep?' He said.

'Oh pundib-la, chyag feb nang chig!' I blurted out.

Norbu flashed his trademark smile.

He stepped inside my single-room apartment, glanced around and went to sit in the single cane armchair presiding over the clutter.

'I was passing this way, so I thought let me see how Bhattacharya is pulling through this cold weather. Bengalis are so scared of the Darjeeling winter, you know. But Sarat Babu was an exception.'

I washed, brushed and quickly made tea. I returned with the

steaming cups to find that Norbu had picked up the book from the floor and was distractedly turning its pages.

'Sarat Babu's Tibet mission had a tragic consequence. I didn't want to tell you about it that evening. Remember?' Norbu said soberly, looking into my face.

'Sometime after he returned, his real identity became known there, and also the real purpose of his visit. The government in Lhasa sent spies to Darjeeling to verify this. And then the arrests began. All the Tibetans who had helped him in some way or the other during his stay there, those who had mingled with him or hosted him in their houses, even those who had lent him porters and pack animals, were tried. They were charged with the gravest of crimes: sedition. Those who were given lesser punishments were manacled and let loose, some with their eyes gouged out, others were thrown into the cave prisons. Lama Sengchen Dorjechen was sentenced to death.'

During his stay in Shigatse, Sarat Chandra had seen wretched convicts, mostly swindlers and thieves, out on the streets.. They presented a horrible sight: groups of a dozen to twenty men manacled in a single chain or caught in wooden stocks, with marks of torture on their bodies. They begged around in the market square.

But the descriptions of Tibetan prisons found in the writings of travellers were truly horrendous. These were actually dungeons made of stone and mortar, with narrow air vents on top. Rotten food and other refuse were occasionally thrown in through these vents, and the exits were permanently sealed. The prisoners never ever got a chance to come out; they didn't need to, because most perished in a short time. But a few of them continued with the living death. The British military expedition to Tibet in 1903, led by Francis Younghusband, had freed such survivors. Among them were those who had hosted or helped Sarat Chandra Das during his stay in Tibet.

More than twenty years had passed by then. After their decades-long incarceration in sunless cells, it was difficult to recognize them as humans. Death pale, skeletal, almost reptilian, with irises turned white like that of albinos, clothes rotted away from their bodies, women scarcely distinguishable from men, they had survived all this time in the lightless cells on moss and drops of moisture in the fissures of stone. But when they were taken out into the light of the day, most died in no time, crushed by the blinding weight of the sun.

Lama Sengchen Dorjechen was drowned in the Tsangpo. It was a gruesome spectacle, attended by the entire population of Shigatse. Millstones were tied around the venerable lama's neck and he was slowly lowered with ropes into the rapids from the top of a deep ravine. He was calm in the face of death and murmuring prayers, eyewitness accounts had said, but the lamentations from the crowd had drowned the river's roar. It had taken a long time to put him to death.

'It's rather strange that the instruments Sarat Chandra was carrying had never roused the lama's suspicion,' I mused.

'On the contrary,' Norbu said. 'He was learning land survey techniques from his young civil engineer friend, and also the techniques of photography. He was even writing a book on this in Tibetan. During the period Das was in Tashilhunpo to study the rare manuscripts, Lama Sengchen took lessons from him in English and Physics. He had procured through him a telescope that he used to study the stars and also a magic lantern to view the scenes of the world.'

Norbu paused, took a deep breath and looked at me. He continued: 'You know Bhattacharya, the more I think on this the more a thought takes root in my mind. The great Sengchen's irrepressible fascination with Western science had clouded his judgement about Sarat Chandra and the real motive of his mission.'

'I was reading his words that Sarat had quoted in the book,' I said. 'I want the door of the world to open, Sengchen is saying, the winds of time to enter our land. And that door is in India. The new age will come through the land from where Lord Buddha's words have come. That's what he is saying, or something like that.'

Norbu nodded his head gravely, his eyes fixed on the capillaries of mist on the glass panes, showing a sunny morning outside. He said softly: 'Yes, and had his dreams come true, Francis Younghusband would have discovered a completely different Tibet.'

'Or perhaps none at all,' I added. 'Perhaps there'd have been no need to launch a military expedition.'

What did Sarat read in Rinpoche's palm on that night of wind and moon? She never had the chance to see again the green valleys of her home. It was never known what happened to her; if she, too, had been thrown into the cave prison along with her in-laws, if she was among the wretched creatures set free after twenty years.

Other than Rinpoche, Sarat Chandra became familiar with another woman during his stay in Tibet. She was a Lhacham, a princess, the thirty-something wife of a wealthy and influential man. Their first meeting left a deep impression in his mind. She was dressed in a Mongol robe, made from the richest Chinese satin brocades and the finest native cloth; pearl necklaces, strings of amber and coral hung over her breast and on her head she wore a crown studded with precious stones and pearls of every size.

She had caught cold in Shigatse and was suffering from lung inflammation. Sarat had cured her. He carried a box of biochemical medicines for his personal needs, but he had administered them to many people during his stay in Tibet. This had helped spread his fame as a pundit who'd mastered different branches of knowledge. But Lhacham's was a special case, as her ailment had been complicated by an overdose of medicines. After Sarat found this out, the only medicine he prescribed her was a placebo, or no medicine at all; and she began to respond quickly to this line of treatment.

By curing Lhacham, Sarat earned something more than fame: an opportunity to accompany the princess's entourage returning to Lhasa and be her guest there. In fact, since his first visit to Shigatse two years earlier, he had been nursing the dream—the ultimate dream of all the explorers in Tibet—of a visit to the forbidden city of Lhasa. This dream had been kindled during his stay in Tashilhunpo as the minister's guest. Lhasa was about 200 miles from Shigatse, across rugged terrain infested with brigands. Travelling with the Lhacham ensured safety and, on top of it, a place to stay at Lhasa.

Sarat prepared for the journey; he ordered for himself winter clothes that included a coat made from the hide of several lambs. It was the month of May, spring had arrived in the valleys, but there was a chance of snowfall on the vast desolate plateau across which the road passed.

On the day he set off, Sarat went to Sengchen Lama to receive his blessings. He found the lama seated on the carpeted floor, absorbed like a child with the parts of a daguerreotype camera laid out on a low desk. The room was long and bare, with honeycombed shelves stuffed with rolls of manuscripts from floor to ceiling. A balcony on one side had a saffron plant in an earthenware pot. The room glowed in the morning light reflected off the gilt domes of the lamasery. The lama was dressed in a bright yellow robe; it appeared as if he was enveloped in flames.

This was the image of Sengchen Dorjechen that Sarat would carry back to India, to recall during his lonely hours in Lhasa Villa. He bowed and offered the holy man a silk scarf. Sengchen leaned forward across the desk and touched the young man's head with both his hands.

'Sarat Chandra, Lhasa is not a good place,' he spoke slowly. 'The people there are not like those you meet here. The Lhasa people are suspicious and insincere. You don't know and cannot read their character. I advise you not to stay long in one place there. The Lhacham Kusho is a powerful personage in Lhasa, she will protect you, but you should so behave as rarely to require her protection. Stay not long in the vicinity of the Dabung or Sera monasteries. If you intend stay long in Lhasa, find a place in a garden or a village in the suburbs. You have chosen a very bad time for your pilgrimage, smallpox is raging all over central Tibet. But you'll return safely, though the journey will be trying and fraught with great difficulties.'

Lhosar, the Tibetan New Year, had begun at the end of February; the wind had grown less fierce since then. The poplars and willows that lined the road wore new foliage, wild bushes on the water's edge had turned scarlet with flowers, the sheep cropped new grass in the meadows. The valley floors were covered in chequered greens, teeming with busy peasants and their yaks caparisoned with dyed wool and cowrie shells. Ducks paddled in the lakes and creeks under a deep blue sky. Amid such dazzling profusion of life, the news of plague seemed like the figment of a sick imagination. The road to Lhasa was kutcha and rough, at places 20 feet wide but often a trail across the fields or the dry beds of irrigation canals. People travelled on foot, on mules and ponies; the wheeled carriage was unheard of in this land.

Lhacham was riding a white pony. Gorgeously attired in satin and silk, she appeared before Sarat like a heroine in a romance. The villages and farmlands wheeled slowly away as they moved on under the immense canopy of sky. The ruins of ancient monasteries could be seen on distant hills and miniature yaks grazing on grey-green slopes dragging their elongated shadows. The party came to a row of stone shelters of Dokpa grazers and stopped for refreshments.

'Why don't you ride a sedan chair?' Sarat asked Lhacham. 'They are much more comfortable than saddle horses.'

'You mean the ones carried by men?' Lhacham asked.

'Yes, four or more men. There are also covered palanquins.'

Lhacham smiled. 'But is it right to use humans as beasts of burden? Our people will resent this. Only four persons may use sedan chairs in Tibet. They are the Dalai Lama, the Panchen Lama, the Amban and the Regent.'

The path went over a gentle pass and wound along a green valley watered by snow-fed streams. Before evening they came to a village by a lake. It was a cluster of reed huts and large hidebound coracles upturned on the bank, a fisherman's village. They bought tsamba and fresh butter. They abstained from fish because of the smallpox epidemic.

The next morning, the party crossed a river issuing out of the lake. The path followed the river for some distance and then ascended the lofty plateau of Karo La. After a climb of two hours, snow-capped mountains appeared into view. The boundless flat top of the plateau was scarred by a network of streams where soporific yaks grazed. Beyond Karo La, the path again descended a few miles until it reached the village of Ring-la, by a river flowing north to meet the Yamdo. The outlines of the Samding Gompa were visible in the distance. The lush plains of Nangatsu began from here.

There was young barley crop in the fields and women were busy weeding them. Seeing wayfarers, they came up to offer green barley shoots. Women were also seen working in brick kilns, shaping bricks and carrying them to the kilns on the backs of asses. Earthen pots were being made on wooden moulds; the potter's wheel, too, didn't exist.

They were to stop for the night in a village that belonged to Lhacham's father-in-law. Stepped fields were cut on hill slopes with the dzong sitting on top. Flags were flying there. On the approach to the village, a tent was pitched for Lhacham to change her riding dress. She emerged from it wearing fine silk and a gem-studded head-dress, looking gorgeous in the mellow late afternoon sun that in Bengal is called the 'kaney dekha alo', the light for viewing the new bride.

Sarat inquired about the custom of polyandry.

'Don't men in India marry multiple women?' Lhacham retorted.

'Not everyone, but the custom is there,' Sarat replied.

'How odd! Aren't the husband's love and wealth divided that way?' There was a touch of genuine amazement in her voice.

'But the firangis are strictly monogamous,' Sarat added.

'That is even more odd!'

'Why so?' Sarat asked. 'A person has only one body and soul, a marriage is a bond between the two souls. Isn't it?'

'But brothers born in a mother's womb are part of a single, indivisible life. The same lifeblood flows in their veins,' Lhacham said self-assuredly.

'That means there is no problem if blood sisters marry the same man?'

Lhacham fell silent. 'Maybe,' she said finally. 'But I think Tibetan women are much happier. Their lives are fuller in all respects.'

On the village's boundary, they witnessed a bizarre scene: lambs were being taken to the slaughter shed to be roasted alive. The carcasses, known as pagra, were preserved for months. Sarat had bought such a smoked sheep carcass from a village on their way to Nango La. Wealthy Tibetan households had rooms where dozens of pagras hung like corn cobs during the long winter months, Lhacham said. From a high road, they saw the animals quietly filing out from a pen below to a barn in the distance. A thin column of smoke was rising from the windowless building. The murmur of a nearby spring and the Mani wheels turning in it were the only sounds that could be heard from the height.

A platform covered with a red carpet had been set up at the gate of the dzong. Lhacham alighted from her horse directly onto it. After the welcoming ceremony was over, they learnt that a brother and a nephew of the dzongpon were suffering from smallpox. A pair of lamas were furiously chanting prayers, accompanied by a cacophony of bells and cymbals, to drive away the disease.

That evening Sarat had a fever, accompanied by a hacking cough. By next day it became clear that he was not in a state to travel. So it was decided that Lhacham would advance with her entourage and Sarat would stay back with his two personal grooms and proceed when he recovered.

The following morning, before she set off, Lhacham came to see Sarat. As he watched her from his sickbed, her face, unadorned and bathed in the soft morning light, appeared delicate and beautiful.

Lhacham placed her palm on Sarat's brow.

'A well-known physician resides in nearby Samding Gompa,' she said. 'It's a monastery of women monks. The abbot, Dorje Phagma, is my relative. I'll write to her and arrange for your treatment there. It grieves me to leave you like this, Pundit. But it can't be helped. I must reach Lhasa before the birth anniversary of our great Lord. There will be a big ceremony in our house, people will come from faraway places. My doors will always be open for you in Lhasa.'

Dorje Phagma, the Thunderbolt Sow, was a reincarnated female monk. Samding Gompa sat atop a low hill upon a bare plateau. The path to it went around a lake. Sarat's grooms wrapped him in blankets, put a turban on his head, sunglasses to cover his inflamed eyes, and set him on a pony. Riding on it for some distance his fever-wracked body went limp, and they had to tie him to the saddle. Each breath of the icy wind lacerated his lungs. At one place he saw a flock of eagles roosting on crags and a pair of men in white clothes and turbans working on something on a stone terrace. They were cutting up human cadavers into small pieces and laying them on the stone. This funeral custom was known as jhator—the offering to the birds, the sky burial. The scene was dyed in the midnight blue of his sunglasses.

A flight of steps cut into the hillside rose to the monastery's gate. As Sarat dragged himself up it, sudden dizziness hit his head like a sledgehammer. A porter had to be found to carry him in a basket to the top. As their sick master waited outside the gompa's gate, one of the grooms took Lhacham's letter inside. Two fierce Yamdo watchdogs chained to the gate post growled at the human figure swaddled in blankets and in dark sunglasses.

Amchi, the physician, had his quarters inside the maze of the monastery. Rolling a prayer wheel, the grizzled old man, who gave off a smell of snuff, examined the patient: he inspected the latter's eyes and the tongue, asked a volley of questions about the nature of the pain, its habits, the colour and smell of shit, piss and phlegm. Medicines were administered, and lodgings arranged inside the lamasery. Two low six-by-eight-feet rooms, darkened with the greasy soot of butter lamps, were rented for four annas per day. Sarat had also to pay for Dorje Phagma's gifts, tea and alms for eighty monks, and the ritual chanting of sutras to appease the evil demigods.

But nothing worked. Hours and days turned into an endless bog as Sarat sank into delirium. Meanwhile, following Dorje Phagma's instruction, a reed effigy was made of him in order to deceive death. Live fish were also released into the lake. As he wallowed in fever, Sarat could vaguely sense unknown men shuffling about the room, their voices swirling around in the yak-butter air long after they'd left. His effigy, fitted with his clothes and the sunglasses, kept vigil. Someone wanted to borrow his pony to go to the fishermen's village to buy fish, another came carrying a pill from Dorje Phagma containing Kashyap Buddha's remains. The Thunderbolt Sow had read his fortune on a dice, a messenger announced, and had forecast that the Pundit from India wouldn't die, but would suffer great pains. She would also come to see him soon. Strong winds blew day and night, knocking at the doors, making the wooden building creak and groan like a storm-tossed boat. It became mixed up with the relentless chanting in the next room.

Sarat lay tossing, ravaged by nightmares. Once, he saw the familiar face of a woman under the veil of a mustard-yellow sari leaning over him; she was looking at his face with tearful eyes. He opened his eyes and looked out of the tiny window to find Dorje Phagma stretched out on her back against the horizon and her protruding rows of mammaries, composed into a series of mountain ranges, squirting blue thunderbolts. Was he going to die? He thought with horror. Inside this nightmare gompa? So far away from his family and home? Sarat summoned a lama and dictated his will through the thick haze in his head. The winds carried demonic laughter and beastly wails. The noise fanned out to the distant hills and rebounded, and continued to hammer in the veins pulsing at his temple.

And then it all stopped. The chanting ceased, the silence of a sealed cave prison descended over the world. Sarat opened his eyes and saw his own effigy propped up against the wall, facing him, casting a sullen look through the blue glasses. He got up from the sweat-soaked bed and stepped out of the room, his body feeling light as a feather. A strange otherworldly light lit up a narrow courtyard before him, ashes were borne aloft in the air. Not a soul was around. He saw rows upon rows of cells piled on all sides like a beehive, a jumble of hanging balconies and step ladders flying in all directions. He drifted along the labyrinth and came to the entrance of a low deep hall with innumerable columns. It was dark. Sarat stepped inside and brushed against a column: it began to sway. Suddenly he noticed that what he'd mistaken for columns were in fact pagras, carcasses of sheep roasted alive, hanging from their hind legs. He had entered the meat cellar of the monastery.

But the more he tried to get out, the more he lost his way, and strayed deeper into the shadowy forest of pagra, into the interior of the hall where the death cries of the animals were coiled in a spiral of mist and, in its silent centre, hung Lhacham. She was completely naked, pale as death, suspended on a steel hook that clamped into her lower jaw and went right through her cranium; and yet, surprisingly, the pupils of her eyes were moving, her cold unfeeling gaze was fixed upon his face.

A MIRAGE

'My relationship with the Government, whom I served with continued and unswerving fidelity, for a period of thirty-three years, are and have been such, for some years, that I derive solace from the following lines of the famous Persian poet:

> Oh Hafez, have patience, when in difficulties, day and night,
> In the long run, you will attain your object, some day.'

—Sarat Chandra Das, *Autobiography*

Castaway

Every afternoon, an old native gentleman in an overcoat, hat and carrying a beautifully carved stick in his hand would be seen walking into the town of Darjeeling from the outskirts. He would take the road winding up from the railway station, stop before the mailbox at the bend, drop a letter and continue with his slow, well-paced walk up to the Mall, to reach there just in time to hear the drummers of the Gorkha regiment strike the first fanfare at the bandstand. He would stand at a fixed spot near the fish fountain, still as a statue save a finger tapping on the ivory handle of his stick, in tune with the music, until the band would play 'God Save the King'. Normally, he wouldn't speak with anyone, except an occasional exchange of good-afternoons and how-do-you-dos with one or two English gentlemen, old as him, and return the way he had come before the evening darkness settled over the town. Hardly anyone from among the small white crowd gathered at the Mall would recognize him. Those who could would cast surreptitious glances and whisper among each other.

He was a former spy, a Rai Bahadur and a Commander of the British Empire. He was a 'Tibet Returned'. Rudyard Kipling had modelled a character on him in one of his novels.

After he suffered for eleven days in the Samding monastery, Sarat Chandra recovered and was finally able to fulfil his dream, the ultimate dream of explorers in the land of the snows: a visit to Lhasa. Not only did he go there but, with Lhacham's help, gained an audience with the thirteenth Dalai Lama at the Potala Palace. With this feat, he joined the ranks of a select group of 19th-century adventurers. He also visited other parts of central Tibet and returned to India more than a year after he had set out.

Sarat Chandra came back on 27 December 1882. Christmas and New Year celebrations were on in Darjeeling. He returned with boxes full of rare books, manuscripts and thangkas, loaded upon two yaks, that he'd collected from dealers in Shigatse and also received as gifts. Among these were rare volumes of Sanskrit texts that had all but vanished from India. But the most important thing that he had brought back was the diary in which he'd kept a daily record of his experiences. Based on it, he prepared reports that would circulate at the top levels of the bureaucracy in Calcutta and London. Das would visit China as part of the diplomatic mission on Tibet affairs, would be conferred the titles of CBE, Rai Bahadur, and would also win a medal from the Royal Geographic Society. His pretty little bungalow on the outskirts of Darjeeling would become the coveted address for all Tibet enthusiasts across the world. He would set up the Buddhist Texts Society and write his books there.

When Sarat was writing about his Tibet days, the people who had hosted him were being thrown into cave prisons. Sengchen Dorjechen was executed in a grisly show of punishment. Sarat wasn't unaware of these incidents. Goods and news were traded between Darjeeling and the border towns of Tibet. The shadows of death that he'd left in his wake lengthened when his reports were circulating in the upper echelons of the government. Armed with the information contained in them, Britain would launch a full-scale military expedition in 1903. Tibet would be prised open like an oyster. Sealed cave prisons would be broken open to free pale, skeletal humans.

That was in 1904. The final round of the Great Game was now being played out. The fear of a Russian occupation in Tibet, that had goaded Britain to invade it, turned out to be a hoax. The arms factory that Younghusband's men found in Lhasa was so primitive that they didn't have the heart to pull it down.

The British Empire was now firmly entrenched on Indian soil. A railway network bound up vast territories, the telegraph was in place, and now there was the telephone. As Francis Younghusband pushed deep into Tibet, his men laid a telephone line along their route to keep in touch with the mission headquarters in Darjeeling and Calcutta. Motion pictures had been invented, and automobiles, altering human perception of time and space. But the land the British army discovered across the forbidding mountains was exactly as Sarat Chandra Das had described it.

Sarat Chandra Das went to Tibet as a spy, but fell in love with the ancient civilization, its language and culture. Francis Younghusband, too, went there leading a military mission, but the land brought about a deep transformation in him. This is evident in his glowing descriptions of nature there, the celestial beauty of the endless plateau, of waking up inside the tent at the crack of dawn at the bugle's call and viewing the frost-encrusted plains shimmering under the fading light of the stars, the first rays of the sun on Chomolhari top, and the phosphorescence of scarlet, blue, orange and violet during the sunsets. His writings capture the moments of epiphany that he experienced up there.

But the mission the forty-year-old army officer led was, in reality, one of the bloodiest chapters in the history of British imperialism. Thousands of Tibetans died fighting the advanced fire power of the English forces with primitive matchlock rifles, swords, spears and slingshots. The gompas and lamaseries along the route were also ruthlessly sacked.

After he returned to Darjeeling in 1882, even as he immersed himself in his studies and the compilation of a Tibetan dictionary, Sarat kept an eye on the developments that were of strategic importance to Her Majesty's government. One of his sources was purported to be Ekai Kawaguchi, the Japanese scholar, who had stayed in Tibet in the last three years of the 19th century disguised as a Chinese monk.

The military expedition of 1903–04 set at rest a lot of speculation, and effectively pulled a curtain on espionage on the roof of the world. It was from this time that Sarat Chandra Das—or SCD, as he was known in government circles—lost his standing. His books, too, disappeared, pushed out by the cache of books on Tibet that the Younghusband mission had spawned. His reports were buried in musty archives. Sarat Chandra Das's name was consigned to the litterbin of colonial amnesia, like that of many others before him, to be occasionally recalled at the officers' clubs, during the evening round of drinks, as remote and flimsy as a minor character in a novel. In the autumn of his life, his body worn by premature ageing, dressed in an overcoat, a bowler hat and a walking stick in his hand, SCD did resemble a fictional character who had miraculously stepped out of a book.

I had chanced on a photograph of him taken during this time, amid a sheaf of old bromide prints of unknown natives at Darjeeling's Das Studio. It was a faded 7X10 cm print of a thin old man in an oversized suit, looking into the camera from under bushy eyebrows. I didn't pay it much attention as I was then excited about another photograph: it was of a German sahib who had the looks of a Mongolian, complete with a shaved crown and a grey goatee, who claimed that he was a reincarnated Dalai Lama. This was Nicholas Roerich, the painter and adventurer, and the photograph was taken at the Planter's Club in Darjeeling in 1923, six years after Sarat Chandra Das died.

Many years later I saw the same photograph of Sarat Chandra in an old lady's flat in Kolkata. She was his great granddaughter. It had taken me long to search her out. Nobody in the city could tell me anything about Das's descendants. I had read somewhere that he'd spent the last years of his life at Maniktala in north Kolkata, but that was all I could learn about his Kolkata connection. For days, I roamed the narrow lanes of this old neighbourhood in the wild hope of finding the house, or at least an old stone bearing his name, but in vain. The area had changed drastically since Sarat Chandra's times because of its proximity to the city's new business hub. The middle-class Bengali families who'd lived here for generations had left; the neighbourhood was now mostly inhabited by the Marwari business class. I visited the Mahabodhi Society on College Street in the hope of some lead but that too didn't work. Finally, I got in touch with an amateur mountaineering group which had great interest in this spy-turned-Buddhist scholar from purely mountaineering aspects. For them, Sarat Chandra was a man who had broken the stereotype of the effeminate Bengali babu and had scaled the formidable passes, without proper equipment and clothing, back in the 19th century. Members of this group had even traversed

Das's trail up to the Tibet border. It was from them that I got to know about his family, his two great grandsons and a great granddaughter who now lived in Garia, a southern suburb of Kolkata. But I had a tough time getting to meet them, to extract from them any information about the man that was not in the public domain. They evaded me, without being rude, and threw up a smokescreen of failed appointments and unanswered phone calls. The more they did this, the more my curiosity was whetted. I suspected they were holding back something, some dark secret, like the lake of Lachmi Pokhri that Sarat had seen at Gumotang, in whose dark depths mythical water buffaloes guarded caskets of gems. What if Das had a Tibetan wife, a woman he had brought back along with the yak-loads of manuscripts? My imagination ran wild.

But the truth turned out to be entirely different: the descendants of Sarat Chandra were evading me not because they had a lot to hide, but for the simple fact that they didn't have anything to show. The old lady from Garia, Das's great-granddaughter whom I finally managed to meet, was more forthcoming. From her I learnt that the house he had lived in at Maniktala in the last years of his life was a rented apartment, that soon after his death the family had moved to a house his eldest son had built in Park Circus. The son, the old lady's grandfather, had been an advocate in the Calcutta High Court. She had heard stories about Sarat Chandra from her grandmother, but not much else. She had also been to Lhasa Villa once during her childhood; it was later encroached upon. She couldn't tell me what had happened to all the books and manuscripts that Sarat had brought from Tibet. Among the few memorabilia that they had in the house, which she had inherited from her father, was the photograph, a print of the one I had seen at Das Studio many years ago.

In this photograph, Sarat Chandra looked thinner than in his youthful portrait in *A Journey to Central Tibet and Lhasa.* Age had also given him a stoop, but the deep self-assurance emanating from the posture and the eyes were unmistakably that of the young man astride a yak over the Donkia Pass, a sketch I had seen in the book. There was something else in the photograph that one could detect on close scrutiny: a hint of bitterness in the corners of his lips.

I found this bitterness in the brief autobiographical sketch that he wrote in *Modern Review*, a nationalist magazine published from Calcutta. It was replete with a feeling of betrayal, of disenchantment about a government that he had served for thirty-three years. He writes about the slights he had to endure, about the financial dues that were not met, and finds solace in the stoic lines of Hafez's poetry.

This brief, and obviously self-censored, sketch was published in 1908. Das was sixty then, just retired from service, dividing his time between Lhasa Villa and the rented house in Maniktala where his family lived. Part of his daily routine when he stayed in the hill town was the 2-kilometre afternoon walk from Lhasa Villa to Chowrasta, and back. Many had seen him on the Mall at that particular hour, standing beside the fish fountain with a walking stick in hand, his face turned towards the bandstand, swaying to the strains of bagpipes and horns. At the final flourish he would turn back and retrace his steps, down the same road, through fog, drizzle or the golden lights of the sunset.

On one such afternoon of fog, as he was walking back down the Cart Road, Sarat Chandra heard a shuffle of feet behind him. The road near the railway station was desolate, and the fog so thick that objects just 2 feet away were a blur. He walked warily, pricking his ear to the sound of feet dragging behind him. Suddenly it dawned on him that he'd been hearing this sound for many days during his afternoon walks: clearly, somebody was following him.

The railway station was empty, the misty silhouette of an engine and two carriages stood like a phantom train. A stand of pines above the road, partly dissolved in fog, had cast a pale shadow over a row of tilted-up bullock carts. A muezzin's call rose from a mosque below the loco shed. Walking at an unhurried pace, Sarat moved away from the khud-side to the hillside. The person following him, too, shifted direction. Sarat slowed down and looked back fleetingly; all he could see through mist was a short figure in a dull blue coat and a gawky, shuffling gait.

A memory flashed into his mind like a spring-knife. In Shigatse, during a similar hour of dusk, a lame beggar had followed Ugyen Gyatso in the bazaar with loud taps of his stick, had overtaken and leapt before him on the crowded square. 'Philing! Philing!' he had screamed, blocking the path with his stick. The beggar was from Darjeeling and he had recognized the lama. Ugyen had barely managed to slip into a dark lane, after thrusting a coin into the beggar's hand, as a crowd was beginning to gather.

A quarter furlong from the railway station, the road had taken a sharp bend. Sarat quickened his pace, went around the bend and took position, standing with his back pressed against the buttressed hill. The moment the stranger rounded the bend, Sarat pounced on him with all the strength he could muster.

He grabbed the man by the gullet and, pushing him against the wall, wrenched out a gupti knife, long and sleek as a steel serpent, from inside the sheath of the stick.

'Rascal! Mero pichha kina gareko, huh?' he shouted, overwhelmed by the swiftness of his own action.

The man, too, was petrified by the suddenness of it. His eyeballs almost pushed out through the narrow slits to meet the knife's sharp point. Sarat saw before him a diminutive old man of Tibeto-Mongoloid features, crow's feet around the eyes, a wispy beard on the chin and a stub of pencil stuck behind an ear.

'Pundib-la! Huzoor! Mo Kinthup! Tailor Kinthup!'

A puff of vapour touched Sarat's face as the man pleaded in a feeble voice and took out, with trembling fingers, a folded piece of paper from inside the pocket of his grimy blue coat.

It was a letter, written in Tibetan, referring to the plight of a man named Kinthup, who had been sold as a slave, and who was requesting that the message be conveyed to Captain Harman that he would float five hundred logs, fifty per day for ten days, on the Tsangpo from a place named Bipung in Pemako Valley, from the 5th to the 15th of the tenth Tibetan month of the year called Chhuluk, the water sheep.

The man in the worn blue coat, Kinthup, had been stalking Sarat Chandra for weeks to show him this letter.

When Sarat Chandra Das returned from Tibet, Darjeeling was decked up to celebrate the New Year; he couldn't have returned at a more appropriate time. Two years later, at around the same time of the year, Kinthup had returned to a strange and indifferent town. Dark news awaited him. His wife and little daughter had died, his two sons had been taken to his ancestral village of Tashiding in Sikkim, his shack in Butcher Bustee had been taken over. Kinthup had to seek shelter in a neighbour's lumber shed.

The other bad news was equally heart-breaking: Captain Harman had returned to England on sick leave and had died there. Kinthup learnt this the morning after his return, when, washed and dressed in the only clean pair of clothes he had, he went to the Survey of India office at Jalapahar. A new officer had taken charge as the field director and even the staff, too, had changed; Kinthup couldn't find a familiar face. He was asked to follow a clerk into the burra sahib's chamber and there, sitting at a huge table, was a man with mutton-chop sideburns. Kinthup recognized him immediately. The day before, on seeing a railway train for the first time in his life, he had run into this Englishman.

The burra sahib, Colonel H. C. Tanner, was absorbed in a map laid out before him on the table, a cigar was burning indifferently between his fingers. He didn't look up at the sound of feet inside the room. The clerk stood there for exactly five minutes, cleared his throat a couple of times and finally said in a piping voice: 'Sir, we have a man here who claims he is a Pundit. He is saying that Colonel Harman Sahib had sent him to the Tibet region on a mission to explore the course of the river Tsangpo, Sir. Sir, he is saying he has come back to be debriefed, sir.'

Turner raised his eyes from the table and stared, his brow was knitted in suspicion.

'You!' he exclaimed.

A puff of smoke spurted out from between his lips, his deep blue eyes sparkled with irony and shock.

The five hundred specially marked wooden sticks had flowed down the Brahmaputra unobserved. Meanwhile, Nem Singh had died, the letter sent to his address through a Kazi in Lhasa was lying unopened. Kinthup salvaged it and took it to the survey office, but it failed to erase the crease of suspicion on Tanner's brow. Two years passed before an official report was filed based on a transcript of his oral testimony, but even then no recognition or reward came his way. All the topographical details of his route survey, and the names of more than a hundred places and settlements he had seen on the way, were stored in his memory. He didn't have a piece of paper with him—no written observations, field notes, route bearings or notations of temperature and altitude. Nobody was willing to believe that an illiterate hill man could carry off such a feat. Kinthup's story, of four years spent in remote Tibetan settlements, of being sold and re-sold as a slave, and survival in some of the most inhospitable terrains, had elements of a cock-and-bull story.

Sarat Chandra Das had returned before him. A trained civil engineer, Das had carried out extensive surveys across central Tibet and had returned with a large stash of topographic data, draft maps and glass plate negatives. The intelligence and survey departments had got themselves busy with the great success of his mission. Kinthup was conveniently forgotten. The poor man returned to his old calling in a tailor's shop in the market and began to mend a life rent asunder by years of exile. He got back his shack in Butcher Bustee, brought back his sons from Tashiding, and married again. He slaved away for long hours in the tailors' lane, amid the ceaseless whirr of sewing machines that sometimes brought back to him the memory of a spring with a rainbow on it. Years passed and the memory faded; it felt like a remote, opium-induced dream. The letter he had salvaged from Nem Singh's house turned yellow and brittle. Kinthup's eyesight began to fail, arthritis froze his fingers, his destitution worsened.

By then Colonel Tanner had been transferred, a new field director had joined the survey office at Darjeeling. But after the cold treatment he had received, Kinthup didn't have the heart to go there. He had known Sarat Chandra Das since before his mission to Tibet. After its success, the 'school babu'—as Sarat Chandra was known among the natives—had gained fame and was now a Rai Bahadur. Would it be too difficult for him to recommend a fellow explorer, out of sympathy for his plight, for a monthly pension, or some other form of financial assistance? That was how Kinthup had thought.

And that was why he had been stalking the 'school babu'. A few times he had walked up to Lhasa Villa, but couldn't muster the courage to knock on the door. But Kinthup didn't know that the world had changed in the meantime. On that foggy afternoon at Cart Road, when dusk was settling and the muezzin's call for prayer was rising from the bustee below, the man who confronted him was just like him, a castaway in the desert of imperial history.

Prince from Heaven

Sidkeong Tulku, the crown prince of Sikkim, had received his training at the Phodong monastery near Gangtok. He later became its abbot. The French mystic Alexandra David-Néel had come on his invitation and had stayed in the gompa for six months. A memorial hall there exhibited the letters that Sidkeong and Alexandra wrote to each other, and other memorabilia that the lady later donated to the monastery.

After the Singalila trek and a night in the homestay in Martam, Yann and Malee had gone to visit the Phodong monastery. They had planned to stay a few days in Gangtok and then come to Kolkata en route to Thailand. At that time I was working in the government college of Chandernagore, an old town 22 miles north of Kolkata, by the river Hooghly. Chandernagore had been a French colony for nearly three hundred years until 1952, when it was transferred to the republic of India. Yann was familiar with the town's name, perhaps from a history book that he had studied at school. When I'd mentioned my workplace, his face had lit up. 'Ah, *Shyandenyagoh*!' he had exclaimed.

I had invited him to visit Chandernagore during his stopover in Kolkata. But I didn't imagine that he would really come, that too on a scorching May afternoon, and by a crowded suburban train from the city. He was alone. Malee had gone to Kathmandu from Gangtok to meet up with friends. Yann was wearing khadi kurta-pyjamas bought from the Gandhi Ashram and a palm-leaf hat; the heat had given his skin the colour of pomegranate flowers.

I had been commuting to Chandernagore for quite a few years then and knew it after a fashion. That day, as I accompanied Yann down the narrow lanes of the congested mofussil town, searching out the relics of a settlement that the French had built with an order from Aurangzeb in 1688, Chandernagore bared itself before my eyes in a completely new light. There was this wide strand by the river Hooghly paved with pink flagstones, with the row of old colonial mansions and villas by its side painted in regulation beige. The buildings exhibited an interesting mix of neo-classical and Mediterranean architectural styles. But only their outer shells had remained intact; the interiors had been altered to serve the needs of a contemporary subdivisional town. A pub where French cotton agents used to gather had been refurbished into the classrooms of the government college, the garden villa of a governor had become a museum. Only the St. Joseph's Convent, set up by the Sisters of Cluny in eastern France during the mid-19th century, had remained intact; it was now run by nuns from the Malabar coast. Inside the two-hundred-year-old Sacred Heart Church, in the high-ceilinged prayer hall ribbed with thick wooden joists, the air smelt of dry piety and bat guano. In the French Institute the old copies of *Le Figaro* and *La Gazette*, letters, photographs and lithographs rotting inside glass cases, and the odd statues, a four-poster bed, battered sofas, pipes, guns, compasses and other dusty, rusted bric-a-brac appeared to have been salvaged from a shipwreck. The objects that raised Yann's spirit were the neglected, forgotten vestiges of a past strewn all over the town, in *ville blanche* and in *ville noire*—the white and the native quarters. At Burrabazaar, we discovered a wayside water tap made of cast iron with the name of the foundry, Gillet Castres, and the year 1850 engraved on it; the tap was broken and dry. But the century-old clay oven inside Das Bakery was still working. The baking recipes, too, had remained unchanged, we were told. Yann tasted a piece of the crusty envelope-shaped loaf and declared excitedly that this type of bread was still baked in French village homes. He lingered long in the weed-choked cemetery under a blazing sun, browsing the epitaphs to glean stories of exile and loss. Cows cropped grass between the gravestones, a tramp was sleeping under the cool shade of a cenotaph. We went to an old pub on the Grand Trunk Road to quench our thirst.

The pub had been standing since the time of Marquis Dupleix, the Governor General, whose villa on the strand had been converted to a museum. Time was when it used to serve a type of local wine made from ripe bananas. This stretch of the Grand Trunk Road was then called Rue de Benaras. It was lined with villas of the negotiation commissaires set in mango orchards. They were no more.

Inside the pub, too, the trappings of the past had vanished, except a heavy mahogany bar counter. Now this place was the haunt of the seasoned tipplers of town. Soaked gram and julienned ginger were served free with the drinks by a couple of dour waiters with grimy towels hanging on their shoulders. It had the ambience of a country-liquor den. The mahogany bar and an old, sharp-featured gentleman who sat at the till, dressed in spotless white dhoti-punjabi, looked out of place.

It was a hot afternoon and there were only about a dozen customers. We went into the darkened interior and sat under an arthritic fan. In a few minutes, the gentleman in dhoti-punjabi came to our table and spoke to Yann with a smile:

'Nous sommes ravis de vous voir, messieurs. Que préférez-vous?'

Did the taste of French loaf trigger old memories in Yann? He began to talk about his home, and told me that he had grown up in Digne, an ancient spa town near the French Alps. It was surrounded by green valleys and low wavy hills. Alexandra David-Néel had spent the last years of her life in a villa there. It now housed a museum, with her rich collection of manuscripts, thangkas, prayer beads and other artefacts she had collected in India and Tibet. Alexandra had achieved legendary fame in the Western world, and the fact that she had lived in his hometown left a deep impression on young Yann's mind. In fact this was why he had been attracted to India, particularly the Himalaya.

'She died in 1969, the year I was born,' Yann said. 'She was one hundred and one at that time. But the image I have in my mind is that of a beautiful young girl, an adventurer at heart.'

Alexandra, the daughter of a politician, was a woman of striking good looks and the cynosure of Parisian high society in her youth. She had dabbled in journalism and had even been an opera diva, until she married a rich manager of the French railroad company in Tunisia. But neither fame nor wealth could hold her back, because the Orient was calling. When she finally came to India in 1911, Alexandra had reached middle age. The raw beauty of her youth had taken on a mellow grace. She spent some time in Calcutta and Benaras, immersed herself in the various currents of Hindu philosophy, and then travelled to Sikkim. There she met Sidkeong Tulku.

When the Oxford-educated prince met her in Sikkim, she was already a well-known Orientalist. Tulku was charmed by the memsahib's passion for his religion; it brought them closer. In his letters to Alexandra, he always addressed her as 'My dear sister' and signed off with, 'Your sincere friend.' But in the writings of Alexandra, all references to the prince are marked with a glowing fascination. The enchantment of that first meeting—in the forest of heart-thumping prayer flags at Rinchenpong—had never faded.

It brought her back to Sikkim a second time. By then Tulku had become the king, the first Western-educated king in a land of rigid faiths and ancient customs. On that visit, Alexandra went to Shigatse via north Sikkim. Tulku accompanied her up to the border of his kingdom to see her off. It was the month of March. They were together for a few days, the king and the mystic, travelling on horseback along mountain paths carpeted with wild flowers, camping in the desolate Lonak Valley by the side of a lake, far away from the capital and its prying eyes. He bade her farewell near the Jongsang La pass, at 24,000 feet.

They would never see each other again. Barely ten months after assuming the throne, Sidkeong Tulku died under mysterious circumstances; he was probably poisoned. Alexandra managed to cross the border and met the ninth Panchen Lama in Tashilhunpo. Then she came back to Lachen, a tiny village in north Sikkim, and became the disciple of a tantric who was said to have magical powers. His name was Gomchen and he lived in a cave outside the village. Alexandra built a hovel near the cave, under an overhang, and spent three years there. She wrote about the supernatural energies that she had gained during this time; the power to generate heat energy within the body, for example. In fact when the training was completed, Alexandra had to give a test by sitting in meditation under a glacial spring, fully naked, through a full-moon night.

Meanwhile, the world outside was heating up: a war had broken out in Europe, involving all the major nations. The British government in India grew suspicious of the presence of a French woman near the Tibet border. They deported her.

But Alexandra was never a woman to be cowed down, even by an imperial power. She had set her eyes on Lhasa, the forbidden city, where a woman adventurer was yet to set foot. During her stay in Sikkim, she had adopted a fourteen-year old local boy named Yongden. Accompanied by him, Alexandra visited Lhasa. She entered Tibet through the other side, across Burma, Korea, Mongolia and China. It took her twelve years.

She travelled the entire length of China from the east to the west, disguised as a nun, passed countless towns and villages where she had to sometimes bribe the local chieftains for her safety. At that time, the old decadent rule of the Manchu dynasty was slowly coming apart. Alexandra witnessed scenes of indescribable violence, fell sick, starved, and even survived on boiled leather boots. In the endless Gobi Desert she saw a flying lama, lost her way in the blizzards and crossed high mountain passes during peak winter season. She finally arrived in Lhasa disguised as a beggar, a revolver tucked under her bodice. The guards at the town's gate couldn't recognize the white lady covered in rags, her hair matted, her skin smeared with brown paint. It was 19th December, 1924. Alexandra was fifty-six.

She returned to France with Yongden and settled in the village of Digne to write her books. Yongden died in 1955. Alexandra continued with her writing and lecture tours until she died fourteen years later. She was cremated and her ashes, together with Yongden's, were immersed in Ganga at Benaras. She had wished it that way.

On that long sizzling May afternoon in Chandernagore, over pints of chilled beer, Yann narrated to me the story of Alexandra's life. When he ended, the sun had mellowed outside and men were trickling into the pub. They were workers of a nearby jute mill, coming to imbibe their quota of drinks on a hafta, the weekly salary day. Their weather-beaten faces glowed with frank gaiety. The dhoti-clad monsieur was nowhere to be seen, a young man in a red T-shirt had taken his place at the cash counter.

Beer had loosened Yann's tongue, but he still had the aloofness about him that I'd noticed in Sikkim. When I mentioned this, he smiled.

'You know something, the landscape around Digne is so much like in western Sikkim,' he said. 'The same sub-alpine trees, rounded hills and narrow valleys. The house where Alexandra lived stands at the foot of a hill. When relatives came to visit us, we'd take them there. Among the Tibetan artefacts on display inside the house, there is a prayer garland made out of one hundred and eight human skulls. I found it so fascinating when I was a child.'

Alexandra David-Néel had settled in Digne because the place reminded her of Sikkim, the Himalayan kingdom where she found the love of her life. The same nostalgia, or perhaps the reflection of a nostalgia, had brought Yann to the Himalaya. But he was not a seeker like Alexandra. The world had changed; there was no unexplored place left on earth. The spiritual mirage of the hippies, too, had evaporated. It was pure wanderlust that drove Yann out of his home, sometimes alone and sometimes with a companion. He had travelled extensively in Asia and Latin America. After every long wandering, he would return to his home in Digne to spend time with his family and get back his sense of reality.

'The places I go to, the landscapes, the climates, the ways of life...everything so different,' Yann mused. 'You see...how do I explain it...after the crowd, the noise and the heat, when I return to Paris, so cold and damp and quiet...it's like a strange hollowness inside me, so maddening, you know, a l'appel du vide!'

I didn't know what exactly *l'appel du vide* meant, but I could sense it from the despair that rang out in his voice.

'Is it a kind of jet lag?' I asked.

'No. Yes...,' Yann said. 'But it's not a jet lag in time, you can say it's a jet lag in space.'

The beer interacted with the heat and produced a torpor that was not particularly unpleasant. We walked back to the strand and sat on an empty riverside bench under an arch with slender, fluted columns. A marble slab said in French that the arch was raised in 1841 in memory of Dourgachourone Roquitte, a Bengali who had been awarded the Chevalier de la Légion d'Honneur. The river was full, a cool breeze was blowing. The sun's slanting rays fell on the wind-ruffled waters and broke into countless crystal butterflies around the silhouette of a narrow fishing boat. Across the river, buffaloes were grazing on a mud bank under a line of acacia trees. The bucolic scene hid behind it one of the largest industrial slums in the country, Jagaddal.

I told Yann about a classic Bengali novel, written by Samaresh Bose, based on the mill workers' lives in Jagaddal. It begins on a night in 1857, when a mutinous East India Company sepoy escapes the British laws and comes swimming to this French settlement. Yann told me about Alexandra's last wish.

'A year before her death, she had applied for a passport. She was one hundred years old, and she wanted to make another visit to Tibet.'

He said the words softly, looking into the distance. I was trying to imagine Alexandra's home in Digne, whose windows opened to a view of the Alps that had given her the illusion of the Himalaya. Perhaps she had also seen through the mist of memories a prince standing there, wearing an orange brocaded dress, and a cap with a glowing diamond star.

A Pub in the Town of Mirrors

In the refresher course at Shimla's Academic Staff College, we had to submit projects. I had teamed up with Avinash Chauhan, from the Political Science department of Himachal University, to work on the history of the Shimla market. Avinash's family had been living in the town for three generations, he had close access to the business community there. We shortlisted a few outfits in Upper, Middle and Lower Bazaars and made a survey based on interviews with the owners.

We unearthed some interesting facts. The year of establishment on the signboards of many of these shops turned out to be, on enquiry, that of their beginning in Lahore, Karachi and other towns across the border. After Partition, and the uprooting that followed, the men had set up new ventures in Shimla, sometimes changing the nature of business, but almost always sticking to the old names and years of establishment. Chubby, middle-aged Nilesh Mehra, the proprietor of Daulatram and Sons, grew nostalgic as he showed us a black-and-white photograph of their old shop in Lahore's Ichhra Bazaar, a tiny wayside stall stacked up with bales of cloth under a striped canvas awning. Now it was a glitzy apparel showroom on Mall Road; only the year on the glow sign had remained frozen at 1901. Nilesh's grandfather Daulatram had started the business in the year Queen Victoria died, his father Manikchand used to come every summer at Shimla with a mule caravan. He did business from a rented stall near Scandal Point. A big household appliances shop stood there now. On the spot where Daulatram and Sons stood, there had been a carpet shop owned by one Mr. Pathan (Mehra couldn't, or wouldn't, recall his first name). When he vacated the premises following Partition, Manikchand took possession and hung up the old signboard of their shop in Ichhra Bazaar. This way a line was maintained, bypassing a fissure of history, a hidden narrative painted on the signboards on Mall Road, connecting the cities of Lahore, Karachi, Multan and Shimla.

Scandal Point, the best-known spot in Shimla, also had a narrative. We found this intriguing name in old municipal records. But when we searched different sources for its origin, truth turned out to be elusive. Everyone we talked to attested to the apocryphal story of how the Maharaja of Patiala had eloped with the daughter of a viceroy. A few claimed that the lady in question was in fact the viceroy's wife. But after a painstaking search, we couldn't unearth a scrap of evidence supporting either of these claims. Generations of Shimla residents had kept the scandalous story alive with passionate retellings.

In the spring of 1892, as the story went, the king of Patiala Maharaja Bhupinder Singh had eloped on horseback, and in broad daylight, with the daughter—or was it the wife?—of the viceroy from this particular spot. This had prompted the British government to forbid the king ever to set foot in Shimla, and His Excellency, in a gesture of bravado typical of Indian maharajas, had built an entire hill town in nearby Chail. But we consulted history books and found that in the year 1892 Bhupinder Singh was barely one year old. It was a coincidence that he did become a notorious womanizer later in his life. Or perhaps that had given birth to this scandal. Perhaps one could detect in this myth the stirring of a nationalist consciousness that had been taking shape at that time, or many years later, in the warmth that passed between the last vicereine and the first prime minister of India, a very special warmth that blossomed right here in Shimla, in the shadowy corridors and back gardens of the viceregal lodge.

As I rooted around for facts and anecdotes, layers of the town peeled away and Shimla laid itself before my eyes in new, unforeseen forms. At Rivoli Road I discovered a group of Tibetans; half a century after they had fled to India, they were holding on to their uprooted culture. In the narrow lanes around the Jama Masjid where sunlight never entered, we met the Kashmiri coolies whose links with the town stretched back two centuries; their sad, craggy faces reminded me of the situation in their land. At the Bindra Studio, the oldest living photographic studio in India, we chanced upon a treasure trove of old photographs of burra sahibs and maharajas who had had something to do with the town. From Mall Road across the Ridge to Lakkar Bazaar, from Ladakhi Mohulla to the rabbit warren of Lower Bazaar, with its maddening maze of alleys and stairways, all these layered spaces had me in thrall like some potent narcotic. Until I was stung by the blue felt-bound book.

But any type of intoxicating substance was strictly forbidden inside the guest house of the Academic Staff College. This, and the pure vegetarian food served there, had made the life of some of the participants thoroughly miserable, particularly that of T.P. Marak. Marak taught Sociology in the North Eastern Hill University in Shillong; he belonged to the Garo tribe. We had visited a bar on the Ridge together a couple of times, but it had always been crowded with noisy tourists. Also, Marak hated the flavour of kasuri methi and other North Indian spices liberally used in the few downtown non-vegetarian restaurants. One day, as I was returning alone to the bus stand down through the Lower Bazaar, I glimpsed at a bend in a lane a cosy drinking joint on the ground floor of an old wooden building. As I passed it, the familiar yeasty smell of bamboo shoots and soy sauce hit my nostrils. One day I took Marak to town to spend the evening there.

By that time, my tramps about town had given me a passing knowledge of Lower Bazaar's crazy topography. A series of steep narrow steps descended from the Mall Road to a sloping lane in Middle Bazaar, lined with bookshops and halwai shops. From there a network of alleyways threaded the compact sprawl of Lower Bazaar down to the Cart Road. I remembered having seen that bar somewhere in one of these alleyways. But that evening, even after scouring the maze for nearly an hour, I couldn't find it.

Marak was getting suspicious. But I was dead sure it was there, tucked away somewhere in the corner of a lane. I could even recall its low, lace-curtained windows, the painted Chinese soup bowls and cans of beer neatly arranged on the window sill, and the buxom yellow-skinned lady at the counter.

The evening wore on as we continued with the search and went deeper inside the hallucinatory labyrinth of tapering alleys and hidden courtyards. It seemed like we were being trapped in a passage by Rudyard Kipling in that crowded rabbit warren where a man who knew his way could defy all the police, so cunningly did a veranda communicate with a veranda, alleyway with alleyway, bolt-hole with bolt-hole. We saw a number of buildings that had been standing there since the author's time, built with rubble, stone and wooden beams. Rows of charpoys lay upon dark window-less rooms, porters' ropes and baskets hung on walls; wizened Ladakhi women sat in the carved wooden verandas above, smoking long wooden pipes. We saw a knot of women queueing up around a municipal tap in the darkness below stairs; they were chatting in an unfamiliar dialect. Seeing us they hushed, but the shaggy mohulla dogs raised a racket. The smell of roasting chapati and fenugreek hung in the air; but not a whiff of soya sauce or bamboo shoots. We couldn't spot a single person with Mongolian features; the men who sat on doorsteps appeared to be Garhwalis or Kumaonis. Their large sad eyes, set between high cheekbones and craggy brows, followed the pair of strangers roaming in the neighbourhood at such a late hour. I didn't have the nerve to go over to them and ask directions to a drinking joint. We crossed a dim courtyard littered with dog shit, squeezed through a gap between two squat buildings and stepped onto the road above the bus station.

The bus station was dark and almost empty. Silhouettes of men quivered around a roadside fire. A town bus with somnolent commuters at the windows was parked by the kerb. The conductor stood by the door and was calling: 'Boileau Ganj… Totu…Jutogh! Last trip!'

Suddenly the memory of the bar we were searching returned to me: it was in Darjeeling! It had stood on the head of the stairway above Judgebazaar and used to be run by a stout Tibetan lady. I had seen painted crockeries, beer cans and a large laughing Buddha on the windowsills but had never stepped inside.

I had to pay for this trick of memory that evening. I took Marak to the restaurant of an upscale hotel on Mall Road. It had soft carpets, warm lighting, honeyed Joan Baez, wine-red upholstery, bare ivory arms emerging from folds of chiffon and accented English blending into the tinkle of cutlery: a different world 200 feet above the Lower Bazaar.

T.P. Marak hadn't seen Satyajit Ray's *Shatranj ke Khilari.* I told him the story of the two chess players, Mir Sajjad Ali and Mir Roshan Ali, two noblemen of Lucknow obsessed with the game.

It is the middle of the 19th century, the East India Company is preparing to oust the Nawab of Awadh. In Lucknow, there is disquiet in the air; disquiet even inside the home. The two exasperated friends leave the town in search of a quiet place to play. Roshan Ali knows an old desolate mosque by a village. They set off for it, but the mosque is not to be found. A village boy tells them that there is no such mosque in the area. Suddenly Roshan Ali remembers: he saw that mosque in Kanpur, when he was a child.

Sometimes the mirage of an old forgotten town lurks inside a town, as in a palimpsest, waiting to lay siege to the mind. Sometimes the mirage of a homeland lurks in another distant land, drawing travellers across continents in search of roots.

The Search for Roots

From Sikkim, after the Singalila trek, I went to Darjeeling to spend a few days there. Since my transfer to the plains twenty years earlier, I had taken every opportunity to visit the hill town. In each of these visits, I had seen it change inexorably. My circumstances, too, had changed. After a string of postings in government colleges in different parts of West Bengal, I had settled down in Kolkata. I had also written a book on my Darjeeling days. After that, every time I visited the town, I tried to see it through my book, through the gossamer of memory and imagination I had woven. I failed every time and returned with a heavy heart.

I had had the same feeling twenty-five years ago, on my first visit. But at that time I didn't have any memory of Darjeeling, only a fantasy. Now, more than the remembered sights and sounds, I tried to recall the feelings and sensations I had during my stay here. That dark feeling, that pull into the shell of the self, would return to me like a forgotten tune. I would tramp the winding paths, along Observatory Road down to the Lebong spur, and come back along Cart Road towards Government College. Concrete buildings had replaced the derelict teachers' bungalows, Professor Norbu had died, many senior faculty members, too, had died, my students had left the town seeking fortune elsewhere. Many fine old buildings had decayed and were lying abandoned. Left to their own in the damp Darjeeling climate, they looked prematurely ancient, with crusts of orange moss on the walls, and the tin roofs spotted with rust that appeared from above like brown cloud-shadows.

The same moss encrusted the gravestones in the old cemetery. The place was as lonely as it had always been, except for the odd amorous couples and drug pushers. A few feet above the busy road, a delicate quiet reigned. Was it because of the men lying under the ground in eternal sleep? There had been a brief shower earlier in the day. Lingering raindrops on pine branches drummed intermittently on the ferns; the wet basalt of the graves shone like the plumage of a Himalayan golden eagle.

I once actually saw such a bird; it was watching me with sulphur-yellow eyes. On another occasion, I had seen an English woman in the light drizzle of a June afternoon. Dressed in a cheap cotton kurta-pyjama, wet golden hair pressed against the back of her head, she was standing before a grave. That was my first meeting with Julia Griffith. The octagonal memorial on the grave oddly resembled the column-shaped postboxes still to be found in old cities, a relic of the colonial era. It belonged to Sandor Korosi Csoma, a Hungarian scholar.

This time I found the memorial had acquired a new coat of paint and railings around it. The postbox of a lost era, what letter could I post in it? What letter did Julia Griffith post in it?

Julia had come from England to research the lost ways of life of a Himalayan tribe. Korosi Csoma had come from Hungary to search the roots of his own race. She used to carry a biography of Korosi in her jute jhola, a slim well-thumbed volume. She had lent me the copy. I could never find out if she'd discovered some sort of a connection between her own quest and that of this enigmatic 18th-century traveller.

Korosi was born in a small town in Transylvania. Since childhood he had been hearing a myth that the Hungarian race had originated in distant Central Asia. When he was a boy, Korosi had a burning desire to find out the truth. In those days, it used to take six difficult months by sea to come from Europe to Asia. The other option was to travel along the long Silk Route, rugged and infested with brigands. But Korosi had chosen the second option. When he was setting out on the journey that would consume the rest of his life, a neighbour had asked him: 'Where to, Korosi?'

'I am going to Asia in search of our relatives,' he had replied. Dressed in a rough yellow cotton garment, he was carrying a small bundle and a stick. He was already thirty-five.

But the preparations for the mission had begun early. Born into a family of scholars, Korosi had learnt Latin, Greek, Hebrew, German, French, Romanian and Turkish languages before he'd even finished school. He went to Gottingen University on a scholarship to study anthropology and theology. He even learnt Arabic, just to decipher some manuscripts that supposedly contained key information related to his quest.

It was a quest into the great unknown, whose roadmap was blurred but the destination fixed: the land of his racial ancestors. Korosi had planned to cross eastern Siberia, turn south and enter this region across western China. For this he went to Croatia and spent nine months there to pick up the Slavonic languages. He finally set out in 1819.

Bubonic plague was raging in Russia, and Korosi had to give up his plan to cross Siberia. From Croatia, he went to Constantinople and took a berth in a ship setting sail for Alexandria. But the plague had spread to that region by then.

The ship cast about the Mediterranean for a safe port and finally docked in Syria. On land, Korosi dressed up as an Asian and took the pseudonym Sikandar Baig. After long arduous treks on foot and voyages in merchant dhows along the river Tigris, he reached Baghdad. There he joined the company of caravan men heading to Tehran. He spent four months as the guest of an officer at the British embassy. He started off from Tehran in March 1821, this time disguised as an Armenian. He travelled along the Silk Route, passed Bukhara, Bamian and Kabul, crossed the high Karakoram Pass and reached Lahore a year later.

'Before him, no European had travelled to these places. And yet Korosi hadn't written a single line about them. Isn't that rather strange?' Julia told me after I returned her the book.

We were sitting in a café in Darjeeling. I looked out at the grey-green mountains framed in the window panes and tried to imagine the places whose names had always evoked the romance of the Orient: Syria, Bamian, Bukhara, Kabul... some of the most dangerous places on earth in our times. The last Westerners who had come to India along those regions were the hippies. That was during the 1950s and 60s.

'Maybe because Korosi was so focused on his goal that he had turned a blind eye to everything else,' I said.

'Yes, focused and driven,' she said. She read out from a letter he had written to his family from Tehran: 'Both to satisfy my desire, and to prove my gratitude and love for my nation, I have set off, and must search for the origin of my nation according to the lights which I have kindled in Germany, avoiding neither dangers that may perhaps occur, nor the distance I may have to travel.'

Korosi crossed the high Karakoram Pass and travelled to

Kashmir via Lahore, and from there he went to Leh. Here he came in contact with William Moorcroft, a secret agent of the East India Company and an amateur zoologist. Moorcroft was camping there to collect information and horses for the Company's forces. Here he chanced upon a letter, written in Russian, from the count of St. Petersburg and addressed to Maharaja Dalip Singh, the king of Punjab and Kashmir. It was the early years of the Great Game, and the contents of the letter were of crucial importance to the East India Company. Moorcroft took Korosi's help to decipher it, got it translated by him into Latin to hoodwink the king's spies, and sent it to Calcutta. He also struck upon the idea of utilizing Korosi Csoma's polymathic talent for the service of the Company.

It was the year 1822, British interest in Tibet had already been roused. But complete ignorance of its language and culture was a big stumbling block. The only dictionary of the language available in Europe, a Tibetan-Latin dictionary put together by a Franciscan priest in Rome, was patchy and outdated. Moorcroft urged Korosi to compile a new Tibetan dictionary, and wrote to the Company government to arrange a grant for this. The grant was sanctioned.

And thus Korosi embarked on a completely new path which would keep him tied up in India for the next twenty years. The mission on which he had set out from his country, to search out the homeland of his race, would never be fulfilled. But across the world Sandor Korosi Csoma would be known as the first European Tibetologist.

'That's preposterous,' I quipped. 'A man sets out in search of his origin, takes so much pain and covers such long distances, only to become a British spy!'

'No, yes... well!' Julia flashed a helpless smile. 'Perhaps we can view this from another angle. The little money that he'd brought from home had been spent, he needed some sort of support to carry on.'

Korosi believed that the ancestors of the Hungarian race had descended from a tribe in Mongolia, the tribe of Huns or Uyghurs. Scores of rare books and manuscripts lost and destroyed in India had been preserved for centuries in the cold, dry climate of Tibet, in the remote monasteries there. He suspected the key to the knowledge that he had come in search of lay there. A grant from the East India Company allowed him to spend five years in the study of Tibetan language and literature, first in a remote monastery in Zanskar Valley, then in a village by the river Sutlej. He began to work on a dictionary and grammar of the Tibetan language, and came to Calcutta in 1830. Here he set about cataloguing a huge cache of Tibetan manuscripts and Sanskrit books that the British Resident in Nepal had sent to the Asiatic Society. It took him another eighteen months. He took up the job of the librarian of Asiatic Society.

But Tibet beckoned. By now he was all the more confident that the door to the land of his ancestors lay through this mysterious land. He began preparations for the last stage of a great journey that had begun a quarter century ago, in another continent. It was February 1842, Korosi Csoma was fifty-eight. Years of hardship and sedentary occupation had taken their toll on his body. Despite this, he covered the 430-odd miles from Calcutta to Darjeeling mostly on foot. On the 24th of March he reached the miasmal forests of the Terai in the Himalayan foothills. Travellers to Darjeeling usually crossed this region as quickly as they could, and strictly during the daytime. But

Korosi spent a night there. He reached Darjeeling two days later and called on the new superintendent of the sanatorium, Archibald Campbell.

Korosi had planned to go to Lhasa through Sikkim. The land of mystery and magic on the roof of the world was already a most coveted destination for the adventurers, and he was very excited. But on the 6th of April he had a fever, accompanied by violent shivering; it turned out that he had been stung by the deathly shadows of the Terai jungles. As he slid into febrile delirium, he told Campbell about his dream, about his distant ancestors who had set out in the misty dawn of time from the heart of Asia. This region, lying somewhere between the endless flat stretches north of Lhasa and the western part of China, was the home of that elusive tribe: so Korosi believed, and he wanted to prove this theory before the world. But the fever kept rising, his appearance became sunken and yellow, and he lapsed into a hallucinatory state, reeling out strange place names and tribes: Hungers, Ungurs, Oongar, Yoongar, Oogur, Woogur, Voogur, Yoogur…

He died on 11th April. His belongings comprised four boxes of books and papers, three sheets, a tin cooking pot and a suit of blue clothes that he always wore.

Was Korosi Csoma really serious about his quest till the end? Archibald Campbell, who was with him during the last days of his life, had doubts. In the official report of death sent to the headquarters, Campbell noted that Csoma preferred to 'luxuriate in remote speculations on his beloved subjects rather than in attempting to put an end to them by discovery'. Many years later, professional ethnographers would prove that Korosi

Csoma's conjectures were flawed. There is nothing in common between the Hungarians and any of the Asiatic races.

'He had come all this way chasing a mirage. Perhaps he'd realized this towards the end of his life. But can we say that his quest was a failure? He did gain something, didn't he? Life is like that.' Julia said, as if to herself, looking out of the café's window at the tea gardens below. It was an afternoon in late September, at the end of the long season of rains in the hills. Across the gardens, filaments of cloud drifted slowly, bringing the lines of foot tracks criss-crossing the greens alive like squirming worms.

AT SHANGRI-LA'S DOOR

'There is a monastery (with seven or eight priests) but no other house at Pema Koichung. The Tsangpo is two chains distant from the monastery and about 2 miles off it falls over a cliff called Sinji-Chogyal from a height of about 150 feet. There is a big lake at the foot of the falls where rainbows are always observable.'

—'K. P.'s Narrative of a Journey from Darjeeling Gyala Sindong, Tsari, and the Lower Tsangpo', *Survey of India*, 1889

'It was so detailed that many people refused to believe it. Those who did believe it sometimes did so from emotional reasons. A man who had been so brave, so persistent and enduring, just had to be believed, the argument ran.'

—F. M. Bailey, *No Passport to Tibet*

Gimme the Waterfall!

At the turn of the 20th century, Darjeeling was sometimes called the queen of the hill stations. Proximity to Calcutta, the capital of British India, and a light mountain railway had helped it gain fame and size. Pretty bungalows and villas had come up on both sides of the ridge, electricity had come, the Rink Theatre, clubs and a race course had been built. For half the year, the hill town would buzz with the lively sahib-mems and their babalogs, busy jhampani bells would jingle along deodar-lined paths all day long, in the afternoon the Mall would erupt with the flourish of regimental bands and the summer nights would echo with laughter and twinkling rickshaw lamps. The age of Queen Victoria had ended, the corset of prudishness had been loosened, the air was balmy with the promise of exciting new times. Englishwomen in India had done away with their crinolines and stays, and had learnt to ride bicycles and experiment with new dress designs. Darjeeling's darzi mohulla was flooded with cheap American-made sewing machines, the old needlesmiths there were losing jobs.

In a tiny shop tucked away in this mohulla, an old tailor had been desperately clinging on to his profession. Years of hemming and darning in dimly lit shops had sapped his eyesight. This had pushed him to other errands. He now went to the bungalows around town to take measurements of the memsahibs. The ladies felt at ease as they appeared in the thinnest of vests and knickers before this doddering old man, who couldn't even read the measuring tape as he held it around their chests and hips, and had to be told the numbers.

But the memsahibs didn't know the old man couldn't read. They also didn't know he had a monstrous memory that hadn't left him even in old age. They'd write down the measurements on scraps of paper and hand it to him, but that really wasn't necessary. The old man would return to the master tailor carrying in his head the numbered contours of half-naked female bodies, just as he had returned to town many years ago carrying the shapes of spurs, hills and forested valleys in a distant land.

In the afternoon the bazaar would fall quiet. The jhampani stand near the railway station would grow somnolent and wait for the 4 o' clock up train from the plains. The bell in the clock tower would strike the hour of three. As the tireless rattle of the sewing machines echoed in the old man's ears, the needle in his fingers would freeze, the spinning steel bobbins would be transformed into the murmur of a waterfall. It was a fall that cascaded down a sheer cliff face into a silent abyss. Clouds of mists billowed up from the depths, with a rainbow shimmering on them, and tiny scarlet minivets darting about to catch waterborne insects. He would wake up from the reverie with a start, it would all seem to be the memory of a past life.

One such drowsy afternoon the tailors' mohulla was roused by the thud of heavy military boots. The busy hands stopped mid-stitch, some even rose to foreheads to salute the handsome young officer in a khaki tunic and a blue silk scarf neatly folded around his neck. The sahib officer didn't look anywhere but strode straight into the lane, until he stopped at the shop where the old tailor worked. Seeing him at the door, the old man slowly rose to his feet, narrowed his eyes as if he was trying to thread a needle, and called forth all the lines on his face. The officer had cold blue eyes, a walrus moustache, and a revolver in his belt. He stood there for a few seconds with arms akimbo, sizing up the doddering old man, and then said in a gruff voice, 'Kinthup, you cheat! Gimme the big waterfall!'

The old man shrank in fear, his face took on the pallor of death. By then, a small crowd had gathered behind the sahib. All the sewing machines stopped and a breathless silence fell over the darzi mohulla.

'I did find the rainbow, but not the big waterfall!' the officer said. 'Where did you hide it, old man?'

Frequent errands to the bungalows had given the old man a smattering of English. He now began to stutter: 'I … Sahib… no waterfall… I poor tailor, Sahib!'

A mysterious smile was fluttering below the officer's moustache, like a butterfly struggling out of a cocoon. Now it burst across his face. He guffawed, lunged forward and took the old man in his muscular arms. He shook the gaunt stunned shoulders and shouted in his ears, 'Tsangpo is Dihang! Kinthup, you were bang on! By Jove, Tsangpo is Dihang!'

The crowd of people witnessing the scene couldn't make out what was happening, but seeing the sahib embracing the old man they clapped enthusiastically.

Now the sahib joined them in clapping. He, Colonel Frederich Marshman Bailey, pulled the blue scarf off his neck and garlanded the old man with it.

The key to the truth claim of Kinthup's mission, the five hundred keys to be precise, had floated away unnoticed along the Dihang-Brahmaputra. He didn't have a scrap of paper with him to support his claim. Four years after he returned, an official report of the Tsangpo mission was published by the Survey of India along with the expeditions of three other Pundits in different parts of Tibet. It was a rather sketchy account of Kinthup's travel, without maps or figures, a litany of more than a hundred place names. It was in fact the transcript of his oral testimony, passed through two languages. In course of time, everyone forgot the illiterate tailor-spy sent to solve the mystery of the river Tsangpo. The report of his incredible mission gathered mould in the department's archive under a mountain of other documents.

But a small detail, rather spare and factual, had slipped out of its pages like a magical butterfly. It had left the damp archive to flutter around in gymkhana circles and officers' messes. It was the mention of a waterfall that fell from a 150-foot high cliff into a big lake, forming a cloud of spray. There was a divine image painted on the rock behind the screen of cascading water, and a permanent rainbow shimmering on the cloud of spray. The site was two days' march from a monastery at Pemakochung, where Kinthup had been staying with the Chinese lama. He had gone to visit the waterfall alone while the lama was recuperating from illness.

Geographers seized on the description of this waterfall and imbued it with the mystery befitting a hidden wonder of nature. It had to be there, they argued, otherwise how could a river flowing at 9,000 feet come down to almost sea level in just 200 miles? The big waterfall solved a geographical puzzle and fuelled the imagination of explorers.

By that time almost all the remotest regions on earth—the

biggest waterfalls and tallest mountains, the deepest canyons and longest rivers—had been 'discovered'. The Sven Hedins of the world had become, in the words of Francis Younghusband, an endangered species. There still were a few places to be conquered, of course—for example, Mt. Everest—but the chance of finding another Niagara or Victoria Falls in the heart of the forbidding Tsangpo gorge beckoned intrepid men like a siren. Frederich Marshman, alias Eric Bailey, was one of them.

In 1882, the year Kinthup was still in Tibet, working as a bonded worker in the monastery of Marpung, Eric Bailey was born to an army engineer and his wife in Lahore. He did his studies in England and followed his father's footsteps by joining the Bengal Lancers. His mad-as-a-hatter interest in the wilderness, and particularly shikar, had earned him the nickname 'Hatter' Bailey in the regiment. During a brief sojourn in the Himalaya, he had picked up the Tibetan language. This qualified him to be drafted into the military expedition to Tibet led by Francis Younghusband. Bailey was twenty then. He had a passion for nature—its plants, animals and especially butterflies. As the troop wound its way through the endless rugged plains of Tibet, a land of fabulous natural wonders opened up before the eyes of this raw young soldier. After the bloody battle on the Karo Pass and the siege of Gyantse, they finally reached Lhasa and garrisoned there for seven weeks. During the occupation, while his fellow officers tramped about the labyrinth of the once-forbidden city, Eric Bailey made forays into the surrounding valleys.

One evening, just after sunset—one of the indescribably beautiful sunsets that occur in the rarefied air at such heights—Bailey met Younghusband upon a bare flat plain. The commander was returning to camp after viewing the sunset from a cliff, something he did everyday with religious fervour. He was riding a horse, a field glass hung from his neck. The vastness of the flats and the sky made him appear smaller than he was. Bailey offered a salute and a greeting, to which Younghusband responded with a nod, but said nothing. The sun had set, but an opalescent light still lingered in the sky. It was getting flecked with stars. Bailey noticed a strange expression of bliss on his commander's face; it was as if the light from the sky had dyed his skin.

'What's that?' Younghusband asked, pointing to a plant in the young Captain's hand.

'It's *Primula denticulate*, Sir,' Bailey replied.

'How d'you know?'

'It's there in Joseph Hooker's book. He'd found the species on the road to Wallanchoon.'

Younghusband came closer and took the sapling in his hand, caressed the oblong leaves distractedly. The light on his face seemed to have thickened.

Bailey would remember that light, that expression, late into his life. Younghusband, too, would remember the meeting on the sunset plain. For some time, he had been mulling over sending a small team to explore the gorge of the Tsangpo, to resolve once and for all the mystery of the river. He put Bailey in the team. Five well-chosen officers prepared themselves to make the final assault on the last great mystery on earth. They were waiting for the nod from the top. The military mission had laid a telegraph line between Lhasa and Darjeeling, connecting the once-forbidden city with the rest of the world. As the men weathered the cold, windswept days, Bailey would go to the telegraph operator's tent every morning. He would stick around through the clatter of routine despatches, all ears for word from the headquarters in London. The machine did come alive one day, but it bore bad news: the expedition was called off.

By that time, the world's leading geographers had come to a consensus that Tsangpo was Brahmaputra. It threaded through some of the deepest gorges in the dense, dizzyingly high folds of the Himalayas and emerged onto the plains of Assam. The same river, variously called Tsangpo, Yarlung Tsangpo, Dihang and Brahmaputra. But a survey of its entire course, especially the segment where it disappeared into the canyons, was yet to be made. In that segment lay Beyul Pemako, a hidden valley veiled in mystery, which would later give birth to the fiction of Shangri-La. There was also the mythical waterfall there, falling from a great height and unleashing clouds of spray, with a rainbow on it. It was there in Kinthup's report.

Did Bailey himself believe in the great waterfall? In the book he would write more than four decades after his Tibet adventure, Bailey remained silent on this matter. Fact is, the vision of a spectacular waterfall dovetailed neatly into the puzzling course of a river, or a series of great waterfalls, tucked away in the impenetrable canyon, hemmed in between 26,000-foot high mountains, waiting to be discovered.

This beckoned Bailey, and drew him away from the army to the political department. He went to Tibet again as a trade agent, brushed up his knowledge of the Tibetan language and people, and read everything that had been written about this land. In 1913, he got himself appointed as the Intelligence Officer in an expedition that was launched near the Tibet border in Assam. The densely forested mountains there were inhabited by the intransigent Abors. For long, the British had been trying to bring this scattered tribal group within the fold of law. Not only had these attempts failed, but a political officer named Noel Williamson had been killed the previous year. The expedition of 1913 was sent to avenge his death and teach the Abors a lesson. But Bailey had other plans: he wanted to set off on a mission that had been aborted ten years earlier.

For centuries, this inaccessible region in the eastern Himalaya had been under the control of the Dalai Lama's government, which in turn had been a protectorate of China. Now, with the fall of the Qing dynasty, the ripples had reached far into these frontier regions. The British government thought it was not the right time to launch an expedition in Brahmaputra's upstream, and rejected the officer's prayer. But 'Hatter' Bailey had been smitten by the enigma of Tsangpo. He had not forgotten those arid weeks in Lhasa, burning for a tryst with the last of the great unexplored rivers, and how the rattle of the telegraph had shattered his dream. This time he was reckless. He gave his bosses the slip and set off with Captain Henry Morshead, an officer with the Survey of India, for the great unknown. It was 16 May, 1913.

A Terma

By the early 1990s, the fire of political unrest had died in Darjeeling. The students who had trooped out of the campus and hit the streets with clenched fists and green headbands were coming back. The fire had been doused, but its veins lay dormant under the ashes. Tongues of flame would leap out from time to time; sometimes there would be a conflagration. As it happened on a damp July morning. This time it was a call for one hundred per cent reservation of seats for hill students in the Government College.

It began with an innocuous hunger strike at the college gate. The authorities looked the other way the first two days, and nerves were coiled like springs. On the third day, mad fury erupted on the campus. Jeep-loads of young men, outsiders all, entered the premises armed with cricket wickets and hockey sticks and began to destroy property. A teacher was caught in the melee and assaulted. The principal hid in his antechamber, inside a cupboard. The arsonists even attempted to torch his residence. An undeclared bandh was clamped on the town in no time. Our bosses in Kolkata ordered the closure of the institution sine die, but also directed us not to leave the station. We were like street dogs on the night of Diwali, stunned by firecrackers, yet not knowing where to run. From the state ministry of higher education to the district administration, nobody was on our side, while in the eyes of the local people we, the teachers, were the culprits.

On one such tense evening, a group of us were returning from a meeting with the District Magistrate. As we neared the campus, we found the area dark and completely deserted. Crickets were calling, torn posters and splintered glass were strewn on the road. The neighbourhood dogs had all vanished. Suddenly, I spotted a shadowy figure standing in the compound of the teachers' quarters. He had a hat on and a neatly folded umbrella in his hand. As our eyes met, he raised his arm and called out to me, 'Bhattacharya, I have a surprise for you!'

It was Professor Norbu. I crossed the road and went up to him, to find a mysterious smile on his face. It bore no trace of the fear and anxiety that had gripped us, his own colleagues, during the past few days.

'Could you spare five minutes? I want to show you something,' he said.

I had noticed that every time there'd been trouble in the campus, most local teachers had taken a puzzling stand. This time, too, Norbu had made himself scarce.

I asked him, rather testily, if he was aware of the recent development in the college. He nodded his head in assent; I was not sure if he could catch the tone of my voice.

'I won't take too much of your time. Just a few minutes.' Norbu insisted.

I hesitated. My companions were standing a few feet away across the road, waiting. I gestured at them to go ahead.

The same sitting-room, the same pieces of carpet on the sofa, the same brass Buddha in the alcove glistening in the glow from the fireplace. Norbu poured milky tea in two cups from a large flask with red flowers painted on it. The bungalow was unusually silent, it seemed nobody was around.

From the drawer of a bureau table, he took out a roll of paper and straightened it carefully under the table lamp. It was a thick, handmade, rectangular piece of paper, of roughly Royal size, with a cloth backing. Upon it were painted dense cartographic patterns in green and golden colours and Tibetan inscriptions in maroon and black. The paper was yellowed and cracked, the golden colour on it had darkened with age.

'What is it?' I asked, touching the wizened surface lightly with the index finger.

'This is a terma, the guide map to Beyul.'

Norbu's narrow eyes twinkled as he noted my confusion. Under the glare of the lamp, his face appeared to be made of wax. Vapour coiled up from the tea cups.

'Bhattacharya, you are now touching the door to a heaven that has remained a secret for hundreds of years.' Norbu said solemnly, brimming with a deep passion I couldn't fathom.

For generations, the Tibetans believed in an old prophecy made by the 8th-century teacher, Guru Rinpoche, of a hidden valley deep in the mountains, a land of the final call where they would go seeking refuge when, ravaged by war, greed and climate change, the earth would spin to its final apocalypse. This valley was sometimes called Beyul Pemako and its guide maps, painted with gold and the bone dust of great lamas, were known as terma. But only the very wise men could read these maps. They were known as the tertons. The termas were usually hidden in chinks in the rocks in inaccessible mountain passes, in the secret alcoves of remote gompas or chortens lost in forests, or between the pages of a volume of a sacred sutra among the hundreds of volumes stacked in monastery libraries. Sometimes the directions to Beyul were hidden in ancient folk tales, in verses, in arcane signs and riddles. But only a terton could read them.

That was what Lobsang Norbu said that evening as he showed me what he claimed to be an extant terma.

'But I'm not a terton,' he said with a sigh.

The first Westerner to have written about the mystic valley was Csoma de Koros, the Hungarian. He had written about Shambhala, a place somewhere in the Himalaya whose descriptions he claimed to have discovered in an anonymous volume in the gompa at Zanskar. Shambhala was a magical valley, eternally green and fertile, where people could live a life of happiness and peace, free from hard labour and diseases, under a holy mountain of pure crystal. But its precise geographical location was not known, and it was ringed by tall mountains whose passes were guarded by snow leopards. People could go there only at the appropriate time, and after the right karma.

Over the centuries, generations of mountain people had ventured out seeking Beyul Pemako. Waves of migration had taken place in the Himalaya whenever a community had felt their existence threatened—by a ruthless king, heavy taxation, plague or religious persecution. But nobody had found the eternal valley. Some had returned disappointed, others stayed back wherever they had reached and had struck roots. This way groups of Bhutanese and Tibetans had settled in Abor country in the 19th century.

In the Dibang basin, in a village named Mipi, Colonel Eric

Bailey came upon such a group. They were Tibetans from the Po-me Valley who had settled in this lower altitude after ousting the indigenous tribe of Mishmis. But Bailey found them a jaundiced lot, sapped of the proverbial Tibetan energy, resigned to living in the hot, tropical climate that was not the Pemako they had been seeking. Later groups had come to this region, led by the lamas, but they had returned. Only these people had stayed back. Bailey and Morsehead befriended them, drafted porters and a guide from among them, and started off on their clandestine expedition to the Tsangpo gorge.

They had planned to follow the routes along which the disenchanted Pemako-seekers had returned, cross into the Dihang Valley and follow the Tsangpo upstream into the Po-me Valley. They had with them rations for six weeks, and the prayers of a local lama who, it was said, could control the weather. But bad weather accompanied them from the start, grim skies and pouring rains, as they attempted to cross the Yangyp La pass.

At 13,000 feet, near the approach to the pass, the guide lost his way in thick fog. 'There will be snowfall,' he announced. And indeed there was: Yangyp La was covered in waist-deep snow. But they managed to cross the pass and follow the hair-raising descent into the Dihang Valley across solid ice, deathly crevasses, and avalanches crashing all around them. Half of the porters had become snowblind and the march had to be stopped for two days to let them recover.

The watershed of the Dihang was covered with a forest of fir and juniper, and teemed with many species of birds, especially pheasants, monals and gorgeous tragopans. Bailey killed them for meat to save rations. He also spotted takin, a species of large mountain goat. The second pass on the trail was the

Pungpung La, at 14,000 feet. This too was covered with soft snow and it took the party twelve hours to cross it under a steady rain. They passed a lake, a deep gorge echoing with relentless avalanches, and climbed down 3,000 feet to pitch tents below the snowline.

Next morning, they discovered the faint trails of Tibetan immigrants. Sad traces of retreat, like cooking pots and pestles and mortars, were strewn in the wilderness and after some distance they came upon three human corpses. The bodies, desiccated like mummies, were in sitting postures under an overhang: their clothes had rotted away and prayer beads were strewn on the stone floor. The stones bore marks of fire. They had frozen to death, it appeared, while they were waiting out bad weather. From here, thick undergrowth had erased all traces of the trail.

At 6,000 feet, they found the Chimdro river valley dotted with tiny villages, patches of maize and barley. The villages were under the control of a dzongpon, who was visibly displeased by the unannounced visit of the sahibs and reluctantly provided them with rations and porters.

After a halt of two days at Chimdro, the descent began. It was the 3rd of June, Bailey and his men had been on their feet for more than a fortnight. Now began the almost vertical mountains, clothed in dense forests, with bamboo ladders permanently fixed in places. It took them three days to reach a village named Kapu.

Kapu sat on a spur 2,000 feet above the Tsangpo, but the river wasn't visible from the top. It rushed between a narrow fold of the mountains, breaking into rapids on its course. Across the gorge, a thousand feet above the bare granite notched like the back of an alligator, began the treeline. Cottages and farm plots sat higher up on the slopes. Morshead climbed down to the river bank and measured the altitude with a boiling thermometer: it turned out to be 2,610 feet. From here, till they would reach the other end of the impenetrable portion of the gorge, there wouldn't be another opportunity to take measurements.

The Poba and Khamba tribes lived in the Chimdro Valley, their dwellings were made of logs and stone. But at Kapu, the settlers were Monpas and other immigrants who had come from the Tawang region, and even eastern Bhutan, in search of the promised land. Bailey found it difficult to distinguish between the migrants and the aborigines. All worshipped the Buddha, dressed in the Tibetan fashion, built their huts of wood and bamboo on stilts and drank more than was customary in Tibet. From Kapu, a march of four days took them to the quiet monastery of Rinchenpong. It stood 4,000 feet above the Tsangpo in a deep forested glen.

Kinthup had visited this monastery thirty years earlier.

As Bailey and Morshead retraced the route of an obscure tailor-spy, fired by the dream of a fabled waterfall, they were also unknowingly drawing a line over this region's topography. This would come to be known as the McMahon line. A few weeks after their return, the Indian Foreign Secretary Henry McMahon would call a meeting at Shimla with representatives from the Tibetan and Chinese governments. The border between the territories of India and Tibet would be drawn based on the survey data gathered by Bailey and Morshead. Kinthup would be found in Darjeeling and brought to Shimla. Bailey himself would take the initiative to find him out in the dingy darzi mohulla behind the Darjeeling bazaar. At last, sitting face to face in the mahogany boardroom of the Viceregal Lodge, the officer and the tailor would draw away the cobwebs of memory to recall an incredible journey undertaken thirty years earlier. All the details that had been lost in the report sloppily put together after Kinthup's return, the unforgettable colours of sunset and the call of birds, the lingering smell of a snow leopard in a dechan phug and the piquant taste of spring waters on moonlit nights, would be salvaged.

But the reclamation of memory had begun much before that, in fact before the two had met, when Bailey was following Kinthup's trail. At every step, he was amazed by how incredibly well the unlettered man had retained all details of spaces inside his head. Four thousand feet above the Tsangpo on a grassy clearing in the fold of the mountain, Bailey found the gompa at Rinchenpong exactly as Kinthup had memorized it. All through the day, it buzzed with the incessant chant of sacred texts as a counterpoint to the chorus of pheasants in the forest. At nightfall, the hoofs of fleeing takins drummed the paved courtyard and the growls of snow leopards were drowned by distant avalanches.

After spending three restful days in the lamasery, Bailey had a suspicion. Kinthup's mission was not just a matter of geographical curiosity, he was seeking something deeper. One balmy evening in Shimla, after a long debriefing session, he would put this question to Kinthup.

'Sahib, every human being in this world is assigned a vocation,' the old man would say. 'A few find it, most don't. They search in vain and bang their heads against false doors. In

Rinchenpong I had this vision. It seemed the Lord had drawn away a veil from over my eyes. I returned to Marpung and the Khen Rinpoche granted me freedom.'

Kinthup's words would remind Bailey of Francis Younghusband, of how, every day before the hour of sunset, the astute commander would tear himself away from whatever work he'd been immersed in, jump on his horse and head for a west-facing cliff out in the valley. Tibetan sunsets would change him inside out, and the man who led one of the bloodiest expeditions in military history would become a spiritualist.

But no spiritual high came Eric Bailey's way at Rinchenpong. The weather, too, turned bad. Under pouring rain, they followed the trail that moved away from Tsangpo's course and climbed a ridge: a steep, relentless climb of about 5,000 feet. With height, however, the damp tropical vegetation fell away to make way for pines and, at a higher level, only dwarf junipers clinging to bare rock faces. Human settlements, too, became scarce. At a place called Pango they came upon a group of men and women chiselling pots and plates in a soapstone quarry. At the decrepit village of Tsangrang they saw Lopas grinding a type of soft wood on stone; it was their staple food. On 25 June the party reached the big settlement of Showa on the bank of the Po-Tsangpo, a tributary of the Tsangpo.

Showa was the capital of the Po-me Valley, a fiefdom independent of Lhasa. The Chinese had attacked it two years before, sacked its monastery, killed its chief and his council. Farmhouses on both sides of the river bore signs of that ravage. A hanging bridge had been destroyed. On the banks were terraced plots of pea and other vegetables, with nettle hedges and rows of peach trees. Large flocks of parrots, doves and ravens fluttered over the fields as young boys shooed them away with wooden clappers. The shadows of the birds flitted about over the burnt ruins, over the faces of the village people. They took the two white-skinned men to be Chinese, turned cold and evasive, even refused to sell them provisions. The wives of the chief, too, declined to meet the Englishmen and sent members of the council, dirty rough men who demanded proof of their identity. And then a rope bridge leading out of the settlement mysteriously disappeared, Bailey and Morshead were put virtually under house arrest.

It turned out that many years ago a Chinese monk and his assistant had come this way; they were counting their footsteps to measure distances and were putting them on paper. Were they Kinthup and that lama? Coincidentally, this was followed by men from the Chinese government who wanted to build a road to Lhasa through Po-me. The people of Showa resisted and killed all the men. The Chinese attack was retaliation.

Bailey and Morshead could proceed from Showa only after a letter of confirmation of their identity came from the Abor mission. Two days' march downhill took them to a lake on Po-Tsangpo that had been caused by a recent landslip. It was in a valley shaded with ancient firs. Now they were in Kinthup country. There were cormorants on the lake, swimming and roosting on the dead branches of tress with their wet wings outspread. The birds indicated the presence of fish in the lake. But the village on the other bank, named Tralung, belonged to ironsmiths. Kinthup had taken shelter here.

At that time he had been fleeing from Tongkyuk; naturally,

his survey of this segment of the trail had been a bit muddled. But his account of the streams, ridges, settlements and bridges were turning out to be surprisingly accurate. Kinthup had reported about one hundred and fifty settlements, many of them just a dwelling belonging to a single family. Thirty years later, as Bailey retraced his steps, some had vanished and many new ones had come up. As he pushed on towards the Tsangpo gorge, a narrative of migration and the search for home unfolded before his eyes, an unending saga that the mountain people had been scripting for centuries in some of the remotest and most desolate regions of the Himalaya.

As they drifted down the still waters of the lake upon a raft of dugout canoes, the surroundings were strangely quiet, except for the clangour of a hammer on the distant bank. When Kinthup had come here, it was winter. The forests above had shed their leaves, the lake waters were raucous with great flocks of orange-headed ducks flying in from the north. Kinthup had spent five days and nights in the jungle before he took shelter in an ironsmith's shed. Holed up there for three days, behind a stack of faggots, he had listened to the feverish wingbeats of the nesting ducks to pick out the crunch of human feet on the forest floor carpeted with dried leaves. He knew that men from Thongkyuk were pursuing him. During his flight through the desolate mountains, he had seen ribbons of smoke rising above the dark forest canopy and human footprints on wet sand by the river. He had seen tree trunks bleeding sap from fresh wounds and blue eye-shaped lichens watching him from the forest's shadowy depths. After two sleepless nights in Trulung, he had hit the course of the Po-Tsangpo and followed it downstream towards its confluence with Tsangpo.

But Bailey and his team left Po-Tsangpo and climbed up to the Rongchu Valley, into an old forest of pines and giant cypresses. The forest floor was glowing with primulas and irises, and also clumps of poisonous aconite. The men snacked on the wild berries that grew here. Many species of herbivores—takin, musk deer, bhoral and Tibetan deer—grazed in the grassy clearings inside the forest. In one such clearing Bailey spotted a type of turquoise-blue poppy flowers with silken petals. They were shimmering in the breeze like millions of blue butterflies. He picked a stalk and kept it between the pages of his notebook. He couldn't have imagined that these wild flowers would charm horticulturists and become one of the most popular garden plants. The blue poppy would come to be known as *Meconopsis baileyi*.

With altitude, the surrounding views grew picturesque, the appearance of the villages also changed. The cottage roofs here were made of flattened mud instead of sloping logs: this suggested a dry, salubrious climate. Rows of apple and walnut trees lined the farm plots and honeybees were reared in hollowed tree trunks. They camped in the village of Lunang.

After two days' march they set foot again in the Tsangpo Valley, to find the character of nature changed. The vegetation was different, the land was arid, and barley wheat and mustard—typical Tibetan crops—were being cultivated. The villagers appeared to be clean and pretty, Bailey noted, unlike the Pobas below. They spoke a Tibetan dialect. Tsangpo flowed at a gentle pace over a wide bed. Morshead's measurements showed the altitude to be 9,680 feet. The earlier one had been taken at 2,610 feet, below Kapu. They had made a wide detour of 7,000 feet of the river's descent, the dark and closed heart of Tsangpo lodged in the deepest of canyons.

In Kinthup Country

Kinthup had left Tralung and pushed on across the steep forested slopes over the Tsangpo, surviving on wild berries and mushrooms, until he had a view of a funnel-shaped valley. It was early in the morning, a pellucid dawn was breaking. The valley floor was swaddled in pale blue mist. The river meandered quietly here, and a village by it was waking. He could hear the faint call of roosters and the tinkle of yak bells in the distance. The snow-clad Namche Barwa towered in the east, glowing opalescent pink under the first light of the day. Below it, as on a thangka, were the horizontal brush strokes of range upon range of mountains. A spur rose on the wide arm of the valley, with a gompa on top. This was Marpung.

All the pain and anxiety slipped away from Kinthup's mind as he viewed the scene. A deep tranquility filled him. He saw a track winding up from the village below to a long flight of steps cut into rock; these reached up to the monastery. A spring cascaded down, feeding a network of channels that irrigated the farmlands around the village. Painted Mani wheels, turned by watermills set into the spring, were slowly rotating. Kinthup forgot the hunger and pain racking his body and reached the foot of the spur. As he began to climb, the first rays of the sun turned the snows on Namche Barwa into liquid gold, the motionless yaks on the green valley began to stir, village women with wooden tubs came out to call them.

The steps reached a wide, paved terrace. Tiny violet flowers bloomed in the gaps between the paving stones. A pair of chortens and a row of wooden prayer drums stood on the left. The main temple was situated at the end of the terrace. It looked ancient and was made of solid blocks of stone and carved wood, painted maroon and white. In its shadowy depths was a huge golden Buddha with effulgent eyes, wide awake. Sitting below the god's feet was a very old lama, his eyes pinched shut, mumbling prayers. Behind him were three supplicating men, three rustics in rough grey chuba, kneeling with their foreheads touching the floorboards. They had knives in wooden sheaths hanging from their waists and cracked feet encrusted with mud and dried blood; a big toe was missing on a foot.

As Kinthup viewed the golden image of his lord, the weariness of the climb was cured and he felt light as a feather. He, too, kneeled behind the men and touched his forehead on the floor. The moment he closed his eyes, the foot with the missing toe sprang into his mind and he felt a stab of suspicion. The next moment, two swift pairs of hands pinned his shoulders on the floor and a third one caught him by the waist. At the sound of the scuffle the old lama opened his eyes, but didn't stop his chanting.

Eric Bailey could not discover the great waterfall described in Kinthup's report; he only found a 150-foot-deep cataract. But it was on a tributary stream of Tsangpo. He also found a spring on the river at a narrow defile, about 50 yards wide, with water rushing down it with such force that the fall was not vertical. A large mass of water hit against the rocks 30 feet below and exploded into a billowing mist, casting a veil over the fall. And yes, a rainbow appeared on the mist in sunlight. This surely was not another Niagara or Victoria Falls.

But this was a place of pilgrimage. People from faraway places undertook long, arduous journeys in the winter season, when the volume of water in the spring thinned. Behind the cataract was the image of the god Singe Chogiye painted on the vertical rock face. The pilgrims would crawl through a narrow tunnel to light butter lamps before the image. But Bailey couldn't see the god because it was summer, and the tunnel was filled with water.

He also failed to find the serene beauty that Kinthup had seen in the valley below the gompa. He noticed that it was green, the effect of heavy rainfall, and that the forests were teeming with temperate coniferous trees. The Namche Barwa, whose pyramid-shaped top Kinthup had seen in the delicate light of dawn, was hidden behind thick mist. The village people, too, were inscrutable. The first villager they met, a woman, took them to be Chinese and ran away screaming in terror. The village chief refused to cooperate and part with men or information. When Bailey asked him about the path that went down to the river, he said he didn't know it.

'Then how do you get down to the river?'

'We don't,' the chief replied.

Many people had died in a recent smallpox epidemic. The survivors lived amidst overgrown plots of land and grazed dzo, a cross between yak and ordinary cattle. Bailey found it a dreary, uninspiring place, a dead end of the world.

At the gompa the old lama who had rescued Kinthup had died. No monk of that time was around. But everyone knew the story of the Indian pilgrim who had been sold as a slave, and how the kind Khen Rinpoche had bought him back for 50 rupees. Bailey donated 50 rupees to the gompa's coffer as repayment on behalf of the British government.

In thirty years the value of 50 rupees had diminished considerably, though. The world, too, had changed. Some of the items of change had begun to penetrate into these remote regions: factory-made clothes, refined sugar, chemical dyes and aluminium. No wonder Bailey failed to find the magical nook that Kinthup had seen: a valley guarded by tall mountains, a rich habitat of rare flora and fauna. Tsangpo, its life breath, flowed quietly here before it entered the inscrutable gorge.

'Only tertons can read the terma, and you and I are not tertons,' Norbu had said to me on that evening of agitation. 'You cannot even recognize the Beyul until the appropriate time, even if you are taken there. The place will disassemble before your eyes. You'll lose sight of the forest for the trees.'

Later geographers have wondered how a scanty mention of a waterfall in a survey report could cast such a chimera in the minds of generations of explorers. Kinthup couldn't read what had been written on the report. The two men who had transcribed and translated his narration were Ugyen Gyatso and Norpu; both were Buddhists. Perhaps it was the image of Singe Chogiye that had played the trick of the imagination; or perhaps it was the rainbow. As the oral narration was put on paper and then translated into English, the details of two different falls became superimposed. A rainbow, or a sacred image, had welded them together.

Eric Bailey was disappointed, but not shattered. He had prepared himself for too long for this expedition to not marvel at the geography and the natural wonders of the region. He was also fascinated by something else. Before the mission, Kinthup had been just a name in an old Survey of India document, one among the many secret surveyors sent to explore the lower Tsangpo region. He had never even bothered to find out if the man was still alive; the thought had never crossed his mind. But day after day, as he followed the river's twisting course, crossed rugged mountain passes and charted hidden valleys, the obscure native surveyor was fleshed into a unique person. The region Bailey and Morshead had been mapping with a troop of guides, porters, mules, tents, guns and other equipment, the man from Darjeeling had charted completely alone, sometimes fleeing his pursuers, committing the complex topography to memory with astounding lucidity. The more he came to this realization, the more a sense of wonderment filled Eric Bailey's mind.

The sighting of the waterfall, or rather the two falls, couldn't make a dent in this feeling. After the expedition, he launched a search for Kinthup, who was eventually found in Darjeeling's darzi mohulla.

The meeting of the Tibet Frontier Commission was scheduled a few weeks later. The agreement of a well-defined border based on the survey data in previously uncharted territory was on the cards. It was Bailey who took the initiative to take Kinthup to Shimla. There the old tailor from Darjeeling retrieved from memory all the details of a region he had traversed thirty years earlier.

Kinthup died three months after he returned to Darjeeling.

A short distance from the Kinthup fall, a tributary stream had cut through a spur to meet the Tsangpo. Unable to cross it, Bailey and his men scaled a rocky incline to a height of 9,000 feet, where water gushed out of a cave of ice shaped like an animal skull. They covered the icy moraine above and climbed down to find themselves at the mouth of the impenetrable gorge. A series of sharp spurs had reached down from great heights almost into the bed of the river, with not even a ledge or anything for a path. They camped here for the night.

The next day was spent cutting a path across the spur 2,000 feet above the river. High above, a faint track was visible: it wound through dark green forests into some great unknown. But the local guide, a cattle grazer named Dorje, couldn't tell them anything about the track. The party pressed on the following day, tracing the contours of the precipitous spur. The Tsangpo was sometimes visible far below, through thick foliage and swirling mists. Overhead, between the high mountain walls, was the pure blue sky and eagles wheeling in it. Movement was painfully slow, a few yards an hour, sometimes along tracks of takin that petered out on the cliffs. They needed to retrace their steps constantly and push on anew. There was no source of water, no sign of human habitation, and their rations were dwindling. With every step, the forest grew deeper and more forbidding. A forest of unknown plants, festooned with climbers, abuzz with the drone of the Tsangpo.

The tall mountains and the thick forest canopy snuffed out the daylight early, the boiling waters below turned into molten silver. There was no flat space to pitch their tents. They built platforms of branches to spend the night; the porters hung their hammocks on trees. The march began in the morning by chopping a path through a forest of dwarf rhododendrons until they were stopped by a forbidding spur cut by a glacial spring. Two thousand feet below, the river leapt across rapids, the trees above the boiling waters were shivering like ruptured capillaries.

Here the Tsangpo had taken a hairpin bend to the south, opening a narrow defile. But there was no way forward across the vertical cliff. Moreover, the men were blistered and raw all over with cuts from the sharp rhododendron branches. With no food and no water in sight, they agreed to turn back.

Two porters had been sent to Pemakochung to buy provisions. They brought back news that a party of honey collectors had been sighted. They were men from the Monpa tribe, and they had marched up from their settlement further down river. Bailey was excited by the news; he wanted to meet them and retrace their path with them. Finally, it was decided that he would press on alone while Morshead and the others would turn back and wait upriver.

Bailey set off with one porter, fifteen pounds of flour, two blankets, tea leaves in a small Kodak-film tin and some salt in an envelope. He forgot to take his pistol. He knew he was embarking on the most significant journey of his life, one for which he had prepared for years, and which he'd remember for the rest of his life. Forty years later he would write a book on this journey, vividly recalling his feelings, see his old (young) self in the mirror of those times. On the second morning of his solitary foray into the heart of the gorge, he lost his camera. There was no photographic documentation; he, too, had to rely solely on memory when he wrote the book.

Cutting steps into the steep stone slopes, sometimes rappelling down ropes, Bailey and the porter, named Anay, descended to the pit of the gorge. There they met the honey collectors. There were eighteen in the group, from a young boy to a man of late middle age, all Monpas and members of a single family. Tucked away in the folds of the canyon were villages that were often composed of single extended families. These men were collecting honey from the dizzying overhangs hundreds of feet above the waters, hanging on ropes or rattan creepers, their bared limbs painted with the juice of some insect-repellent herb. They agreed to show the firangi the way down the gorge.

But there was no big waterfall downstream, they informed him. The course was narrow and deep all along, the torrent swift and marked with ceaseless rapids. Following their direction, Bailey advanced 2 miles to a flat ground above the bank to rest for the night. There was a cave above, on the precipice. The towering mountains had closed in on both sides in such a fashion that if one looked up above, it roused a rare feeling: a feeling of vertigo and claustrophobia at the same time. Daylight died early and a mist settled. It became entangled among the junipers and cast a grim marquee over the river.

The Monpas had promised to come after their day's work, but there was no sign of them. Had Kinthup come this far? Had he concealed the sticks inside the cave on the precipice before coming a second time to toss them into the river?

For six days, Kinthup had fashioned five hundred foot-long batons from hard rhododendron wood. By then his status as a slave had changed; he now was the gompa's property. During the long months he'd spent there—running errands for the lamas, drawing water from a spring below, fetching provisions from the village in the valley and cleaning the temple floor twice a day—never for a moment did he forget his mission. Above the gompa loomed the great mountain ranges, the curve of the river glimmered below like a dagger. One day the ducks began to return, wave upon wave, emerging from the canyon and flying low over the Tsangpo, turning it into a fleecy river of slate-grey feathers.

The winter had returned.

Kinthup prayed for leave to go on another pilgrimage. The prayer was granted and he returned directly to the cave in the heart of the gorge. There he nailed to the sticks tiny cylindrical seals that Harman sahib had given him. He had been carrying these seals all these years on his waist under his clothes, threaded into a string like amulets. He had become used to their weight and the chill of metal whenever he turned in sleep at night. Now he felt light, in body and in mind. From the first to the tenth day of the waxing moon, he camped there and tossed the sticks into the swift-flowing Tsangpo.

There was no sign of the honey collectors the next morning. Bailey attempted, and failed, to find the track along which they had come. It all seemed unreal, a figment of the imagination, or perhaps the fecund forest had erased their trail overnight. He lost his camera during these wanderings and was forced to spend another night on the clearing by the river, under the open sky. The roar of water grew as the night wore on and kept him awake. A thin strip of night sky above the canyon, thickly spangled with stars, loomed above. It appeared like a nightmare vision through the open jaws of a mythical beast.

The honey collectors appeared at dawn. They had been using

the tracks made by takin herds on their winter migration. In places they'd tied rope ladders made of creepers. Bailey and Anay followed the men along, their muscles raw with fatigue, making a progress of a hundred feet an hour. Their luggage, too, were divided among the honey collectors. By now the river had disappeared from view, but its sound echoed through the forests like a howling storm. After some distance, the narrow ledge they had been following tapered off into bare granite cliff, smooth and sheer and without a foothold or vegetation to cling on to. There was a chasm a few thousand feet deep.

It wouldn't be possible to go any further with shoes on, the bare-footed Monpas said. They also didn't have enough ropes with them. The firangi was asked to turn back.

But Bailey wasn't in a mood to let go. He could feel a wild hammering in his heart that had to do with something more than the physical strain. He had had his thirtieth birthday three months earlier, and he knew he was standing on the cusp of his life as an adventurer. He took off his shoes, tied them to his belt and began to crawl around the rock face on hands and feet.

But a shock was awaiting him on the other side of the cliff. The Monpas had vanished into thin air, leaving behind Bailey's luggage in a crevice. There was only the buzz of crickets in the dark belt of trees. The gleaming peaks of Namche Barwa and Gyala Peri looked down from above. Two thousand feet below, in the pit of the gorge, wrapped in a mist of its own making, Tsangpo lay dreaming. Innumerable spurs rose from it on both sides, like ribs in a deep narrow boat, from the keel to the skies.

THE YAK BELL'S CHIME

'I am sorry to say that in this case, as in others, travel tends to dispel romance, and we shall be told that this fabled waterfall reduces itself to a rapid some 30 feet in height.'

—Address of the President of the Royal Geographic Society, appended to F. M. Bailey's paper 'Exploration on the Tsangpo or Upper Brahmaputra', *The Geographical Journal*, 1914

The Bailey Trail

The most immediate outcome of Bailey's mission was that it dispelled the myth of a spectacular waterfall. It also led to the discovery of a great many new species of plants, animals, birds and butterflies—nearly two thousand specimens of about two hundred species—were collected in one of the least explored and mostly uninhabited regions on earth. While the military invasion of 1903–04 had made this region more accessible, the world was still a young place. Bailey and Morshead had even found a couple of new tribes who had never seen a white man before, or had never heard of a country named India. They had mapped 380 miles of the frontier region. A year later, the McMahon Line would be drawn based on the amassed data, a line worming its way on the map, drawn with a felt nib dipped in red ink. The last great unknown would finally be captured in cartographical grid lines.

Except for 10 miles.

Bailey had been able to advance 12 miles more than Kinthup did thirty years earlier into the Tsangpo gorge. It was believed that 45 miles of the gorge had been left uncharted. But it turned out later to be not more than 10 miles, because a team had peeled away from the Abor expedition to explore the gorge upriver. It had found no waterfall.

Ten miles of deep precipices and erect walls of granite, primeval forests alive with fabulous birds and beasts, immense volumes of water worked up into a mythical rage by that most omnipresent of forces: gravitation. There was no human habitation, and no white man had ever set foot there; the world's last unknown 10 miles.

On their return journey through the Pemako Valley, Bailey and Morshead came to Chetang and entered Indian territory via the Tulung La pass. South of Tulung La, along a trail dotted with the herdsmen's villages of Mago, Lap, Pota and others, they reached the old settlement of Thembang. This broad sweep across the east and the west, between the Subansiri basin and the Tawang area, would be known as the North East Frontier Agency, NEFA. The path they followed would be known as the Bailey Trail.

They had started from Mipi in May and reached Thembang in November. In these six months, the two men had covered 1,680 miles, mostly on foot. When they finally came to Thembang they were penniless, starved and had the appearance of wild men. They had been robbed by their porters and even chased by vultures on top of a hill, where they had gone to take a trigonometrical fixing. It was a hill where human corpses were cut up and offered to the birds.

On that crisp November morning, they found in Thembang a vibrant rhythm of life. This was once a big settlement with a two-thousand-year-old history of continuous human habitation, something rare in the eastern Himalaya. Thembang had been the seat of the rulers of the Monpa tribe. Upon a hilltop, inside the high battlements of a castle, stood beautiful painted houses of the ruling clan made with wood and stone. The windows were draped with curtains of Chinese silk, and on the castle doors stood guards wearing plumed headdresses and armed with lances, bows and arrows. Terraced farm plots fanned out neatly upon the slopes below. Brokpa slaves were fetching water in goatskin bags, doves were fluttering in the fields, bejewelled women were weaving carpets in balconies, under rows of golden corn cobs hanging from the eves. A harvest of chillies drying on the cottage roofs gave Thembang the look of a fairy-tale village with scarlet roofs.

When we went to Thembang a hundred years later, we found it to be a derelict mountain settlement at the tail of the motorable road. By that time, the NEFA had become the state of Arunachal Pradesh. Thembang fell within the West Kameng district. The few dozen houses clustered around the road end were made of corrugated tin, built under some government housing scheme. The hilltop castle lay in ruins. Only the massive gate, made of rubble and stone, and portions of the battlement were still standing. The guards with plumed headgear, whom Bailey had seen, were nowhere to be seen; nothing remained to be guarded. Most of the fine houses had fallen away, and a dozen ragged families, descendants of former chieftains who had once commanded an area between Tawang and upper Assam, were inhabiting the ruins.

There had been a new harvest of corn. Old men and women sat on bamboo platforms in front of their hovels and were plucking at the cobs. A knot of men were busy mending the roof of a cottage; women were sunning tattered blankets. Seeing tourists armed with cameras at their doorstep, they offered cowering looks and slipped inside their shacks. Signs of better times were etched on a carved door frame or a trellised balcony, but most were buried under patchworks of tin and bamboo matting. Notched tree stumps had replaced the staircases leading up from the ground. Pigs and poultry rooted about through heaps of stone and rotten wooden beams. A thick dank shadow pervaded the place, and seemed to have stained the faces of the inhabitants. We didn't find any sign of the two-thousand-year-old history. We didn't find many children either.

Our tents were pitched on a strip of flat land below the ruined castle. Once upon a time a great battle had been fought on this ground between the Lopas and the Monpas, the villagers told us. Centuries later this was followed by a fierce gun battle between the Indian and Chinese armies during the 1962 war.

The village headman—known in these regions as the Gaon Bura, or GB—arrived late in the afternoon, riding an antiquated, puttering Rajdoot motorbike. He was a young man dressed in jeans and a leather jacket. He came to arrange for the porters and mules. Next morning we were to set off on the Bailey Trail.

Remote and less well-trodden than most trek routes in the western Himalaya, the Bailey Trail's chief attraction lay in its history. That history had a rich overlay of war and occupation in the last century: China had annexed Tibet and fought a war with India across the McMahon Line. The geography however had remained as it had always been. From Thembang, a trail entered the dense evergreen forest and climbed the ridges, passing Monpa villages on the way. The treeline ended at 10,000 feet and the high grasslands began. The trail went over two passes, Poshing La and Chhe La, and led through the bare rocky mountainscape to the remote yak-herders' settlements of Pota, Lap and Mago. These find mention in Eric Bailey's report. It was an eight-day trek, an ascent from 7,000 feet to around 14,000, with night halts in tents. The entire trail passed through virgin forests teeming with rare species of birds and butterflies.

Also visible on this trek were the famous peaks of the eastern Himalaya, especially Gorichen, Kangto and Nyegi Kangsang. But to view them one required rare good luck, because the weather here remained bad for most of the year. After carefully studying the weather patterns, five of us old trek buddies decided to go in the last week of October. Tents, guides, porters, provisions and mules were arranged through a Bomdila-based agency.

Three of us were from Kolkata, two flew in from Delhi to join us in Guwahati. We had to wait there for two days to get the inner-line permits and other clearances for the visit to the sensitive border area. The majestic Brahmaputra dominated Guwahati's geography as it flowed across a 4-mile-wide bed. We took a morning stroll down the 'beautified' strand. As I viewed the mass of water flowing quietly, I failed to imagine how one could have spotted foot-long sticks floating down the middle of the river. Clearly, Brahmaputra had forgotten Kinthup, and also the gorge it had passed through. In its rushing waves, in the sweep of the torrents, there was already a restless urge to commingle with the sea.

The road to Arunachal cut through endless rice fields sparsely dotted with mud-plastered reed huts and crisscrossed with small, silt-carrying rivers. Smoke-blue mountains loomed in the distant horizon, evoking a strange yearning and nostalgia.

We now crossed a river named Dhanshiri, the steps of paddy, a name that has recurred in the poetry of modern Bengali poet Jibanananda Das. Beyond it stood a dhaba, a petrol pump, an automobile garage and...our car squealed to a halt behind a long congealed line of trucks, cars and tempo vans. Splinters of glass were strewn on the road, the stench of burnt tyres hung in the air.

'Chinta nakariba, iyat enekuwa hoiye thake.' Our driver, a jolly young paan-chewing Assamese man, said as he pumped up the volume of a Bhupen Hazarika song for us. This was the handiwork of Bodo militants, a regular affair on this road, he said in a reassuring voice; the blockade would be lifted in no time.

And it did. An armoured Assam Rifles truck now escorted the convoy of vehicles. Low-lying settlements appeared on both sides of the road: mazaars, neem trees, broods of chicks skittering across the asphalt, lungi-clad men with Mongolian features walking with bamboo crab traps, emerald tea gardens sun-dappled under acacia trees, dark tribal women picking leaves. So many tribes and communities from so many regions. Under the vast open skies, against the flat blazing shades of green, the tin-and-reed dwellings appeared flimsy and evanescent. It was as if they had materialized in the wink of an eye and would vanish into thin air before the next one. Was the disquiet born out of this tentative appearance of cohabitation?

Near Bhalukpong, the Himalaya turned out in clear outlines for the first time. There was the checkpost and the barbed wire. Beyond lay the land of the rising sun.

I was doing the Bailey Trail trek because I was obsessed with a few characters in a chapter of colonial history. But there was also a private reason. Since childhood I'd been fed with stories of NEFA, of its magical forests and the birds, beasts and butterflies that inhabited them. Dadu, my grandfather, had started his career as a junior postal clerk in Shillong, then the headquarters of NEFA. He'd often tell me stories about a post office that had been set up to serve a single village comprising a single household unit. There were many such single-house villages perched on the remote mountaintops there, Dadu would narrate, so small that a little girl could easily cover it on one foot playing hopscotch. But she couldn't, because there never were enough players to play it. And yet there lived people who received letters. Even twenty years after Independence, many didn't know that the British had left and that India was a free country.

NEFA was for me more than a geographical space; it was a metaphor of the unknown, the unknowable—a private Shangri-La. Its mystery had deepened with the news of periodic discoveries of new languages, birds and insects.

But after we crossed the checkpost and hit the road that climbed up the mountain, my imagination began to fade and was soon lost under a different narrative. This was the narrative of the Indian nation, being written with granite, steel, corrugated iron, barbed wire and letters stencilled in tar. The green armoured truck that had been escorting us from the Bodo-dominated areas had a slogan painted on its side—ACCESS TO JUSTICE FOR ALL. On entering Arunachal, we found these trucks worming up and down the mountains, hogging road space. Military barracks sprawled across the hillsides like olive-green towns. As our Bolero laboured up the road in the wake of an endless army convoy, we peered out into these barracks—neat lanes, basketball courts, red-flagged Hanuman shrines and hefty, hairy North Indian men milling about. For hundreds of years, this had been pristine mountain country where the murmur of the Kameng rushing down below was answered by the song of crickets and the occasional boom of a gompa's horns. Now the mountains echoed with bhajans and the recorded chants of the Gayatri Mantra belted out from loudspeakers.

Near Tenga, a different kind of shrine had come up on the wayside: a memorial for the soldiers who had died on this spot during the 1962 war. The names of the dead jawans and rousing epitaphs for them were etched on polished granite. Standing barefoot on the freezing grass (a notice directed the visitor to talk off footwear), I failed to imagine how the place had been half a century ago, how the hapless young men had died like flies without proper weapons and winter clothing. The harrowing details were not written on stone, but something entirely different. The flowery English and the bold lettering seemed to bark out in a tone of parade-ground command, with veins sticking out at the neck, a sad and embarrassing chapter in the history of independent India.

The entire 45-mile stretch from Bhalukpong to Bomdila bristled with government orders, slogans, warnings and other narrations of the nation. Every bend in the road greeted us with the regulation humour of the Border Roads Organization: 'DRIVE ON HORSEPOWER, NOT ON RUM POWER', 'LET YOUR INSURANCE POLICY MATURE BEFORE YOU'; some were risqué: 'DARLING, I LIKE YOU BUT NOT SO FAST' and, 'BE GENTLE ON MY CURVES!' But the award for the best sarkari wit must go to: 'PEEP, DON'T SLEEP!' A sleepless yellow earthmover stood by the notice board.

The road was being widened: the mountains were being blasted open, the primaeval forests growing upon them stripped away, their brittle gneiss and clay being gouged out, the capillaries of their springs ripped out. The air was choking with dust. From a distance, the rattle of drilling machines mimicked the call of crickets until they were drowned by the drone of army choppers overhead. We passed a number of miserable dust-coated villages. Women and children were fetching water from distant sources; all the nearby springs had dried up. Not an unfamiliar sight in the Himalaya, but here it appeared as if the life of man in nature had been pulled inside out. The veins of an age-old ecosystem had been laid bare, broken open with a sledgehammer.

Coolie gangs from North India had built their shacks on the wayside with flattened tar drums. Their work followed a primitive method: melting bitumen over a fire of green logs cut from the surrounding forests and ladling them manually upon the surface of the road. We spotted a number of cenotaphs commemorating the jawans and havildars of the Border Roads Organisation who had lost their lives building the road. (None for the nameless coolies, of course.) A large notice board before an unusually straight and wide stretch of road claimed: 'In 2008 a fighter jet shall land here.' Three years on, no fighter jet had landed. The part of the road, still under construction, had liquid mud streaming down it after a brief shower. Skidding dangerously over it, rattling across stone chips and pebbles, our four-wheel-drive reached Bomdila late in the evening after fourteen hours on the road. Next day, we drove 27 miles to Thembang.

Thembang, as described earlier, didn't appear to be the gateway of an adventure trail. It was the end of the motorable road, the tail of a foul creek that had carried urban detritus and deposited here: outmoded Rajdoot motorbikes and Mahindra jeeps rusting by the wayside, MP3 players belting out Hindi film songs, and a lot of plastic goods. An ancient mendong crouched at the road end like a mythical animal—paint-peeled, crumbling, and with tiny alcoves for butter lamps that were like empty, cobwebbed eyes.

I had seen that same empty look in the eyes of a group of young local men at Bomdila bazaar earlier that morning. They were all well dressed and lounging on the terrace of a pub, their feet, shod in imported sneakers, propped up on the railing, gazing listlessly at the street scene below. Behind them, inside a darkened room, another group was gathered around a lighted pool table. Their faces appeared like masks suspended in the air, swaying with the thwack of the ricocheting balls.

From Thembang we trekked to Lagam, at 9,000 feet, via Semnak. I couldn't sleep at night. This was perhaps due to the altitude, or the stuffy air inside the tent. Snatches of the scenes I had seen on the road the day before flashed inside my closed, sleepless eyes. I had seen a Sikh jawan guarding a culvert with his back turned to the road, an AK-47 in his hand, keeping a rapt watch on the lonely forest floor. The chestnut trees were shedding leaves, sunlight streamed in through the branches and striped his shoulders. I had not seen his face. At a bend in the road, before the tar-drum hovel of a road worker, I had seen a young woman sitting alone on her haunches with a baby in arms. It was the hour of dusk, our vehicle's headlight flashed on her, the long cold forest night lay ahead. Her keen animal eyes became mixed up with the memory of another pair of eyes I had seen long ago under similar flashing lights of a car, and, together, they lacerated my sleep.

Nimden, our guide, complained in the morning that he too couldn't sleep. Someone must have burned onion skin or plastic, he rued; the foul stench had attracted the evil spirits of the forest. They'd shaken Nimden's tent throughout the night, he claimed.

Nimden was a lively young man with a wiry frame and prematurely rugged face; he belonged to the Monpa tribe. He knew four languages and had taken part in a number of expeditions, ranging from that of European mountaineers to Indian army officers. He constantly reminded me of Phurchung.

From Thembang, an easy dirt path ran along the green mountainside, and passed the villages of Gunthung and Pangma. These were the settlements of shepherds, with patches of farmland cleared inside the forest. Cherry peppers and a type of wild fruit shaped like star anise were drying on cottage roofs, and strips of meat on clotheslines. The women wore heavy metal earrings, nose studs and headdresses; the men sported long pony-tailed hair and sheathed knives on their waists. All were Monpas. Here, too, they didn't cast curious or welcoming looks at us, but went on with their daily work: we saw them pressing corn on wooden mortars, and weaving wall matting from strips of bamboo. The crossed pattern of weaving, of a single weft after four warps, was familiar; I had seen them in rural West Bengal.

Pangma was a village of twenty cottages with a primary school. An ancient gompa made entirely of wood stood in Semnak. The trail climbed up from here. In a small forest clearing at the end of the village, standing on stilts, a lone leaf-thatched hut had the appearance of a bird cage. There was a pig pen around the stilts, and on the high platform crouched a mastiff, coal black and as large as a bear. The patch of forest had recently been cut but the shrubs were yet to be cleared. Seeing us, the dog began to emit a low rattle and alerted a thick-boned woman who stepped out from inside on to the platform. She had a full figure wrapped in a piece of red cloth tied at the shoulder, and legs bared up to the thighs. She watched us with large, mysterious eyes.

I was struck by a feeling of déjà vu. Where had I lived this moment?

Remembrance came like a shaft of light through a gap in the clouds. I had read about such a scene in George Bogle's diary. On entering Bhutan from the kingdom of Cooch Behar, he had halted at a cottage like this. It belonged to the village chief. A trader woman was staying there with him. She had on a single woollen shawl pinned to the shoulder with a brooch, a set of fine teeth and, as Bogle had noted, 'eyes like Rubens' wife'. This picture had been buried under sheaves of papers inside a chest in a Scottish country house, to resurface a century later in the imagination of a Bengali schoolmaster. Another hundred and thirty years later the image came to life before my eyes. In no time, the sense of travelling in a remote frontier vanished from my mind. It felt as if I had arrived at some forgotten centre of my own consciousness, at the crossroads of memory and imagination.

Thungri was a windswept village of yak-herders at 10,000 feet. The trail to Lagam left the scatter of wooden dwellings and wound up around little plots of maize and turnips fenced with stones, till it entered a dark forest. Soon the damp shadowy primaeval world of vegetation devoured us. Moisture from the branches dripped overhead, the feet sank into soft leaf humus. A thick silence, not even the sound of footsteps; only the whizz of laboured breath and the metallic drone of unseen insects.

'This is not the birding season,' Nimden said. 'But you'll see butterflies where sunlight enters the forest.'

There was no path through this forest. Earlier in the morning, when we were having breakfast, the mule driver with his pair of animals and the porters had set out with the tents and other luggage. We had been making our way in the forest by following their footprints and mule droppings. We caught up with them after two hours of steady climbing. The silent porters were trudging up in slow motion, the straps of their loads went round their foreheads like hoods. Pencils of sun pierced the dense canopy of leaves and dappled the steaming backs of the pack animals with bleeding, leech-stung haunches.

The villages I had seen around the trek routes in Garhwal and Kumaon were mostly nestled in the slopes. But the Bailey Trail traced the crests of ridges, the watersheds, with scattered yak-herder settlements on top. At 12,000 feet, we left the rainforest and came to rolling grasslands. These were the chowrikhang, the grazing grounds of yaks. Giant conifers stood sparsely here, and the ravines below were covered with dark green vegetation. We spotted a number of cairns atop the ridges, smooth stones stacked up in neat piles. They appeared like strange religious relics.

'These were put up by Bailey Saab when he came this way,' Nimden said. 'They've been standing ever since. Now they help the army patrol find their bearings. The border is not far. You can see the mountains of Tibet on a clear day.'

But it was not a clear day. A murky fog hung around us. Before we'd reached Thungri, the daylight dimmed, though it was only 2.30 in the afternoon. We were in the easternmost part of the country, but even that couldn't explain the untimely gloom. Thick nimbus whipped up overhead, and in the weak light that filtered through it, a dozen desolate cottages appeared on the brow of the hill. Smoke rose from the low slate roofs, men were busy chopping dead wood collected from the forests below, three women in rough woollen gowns stepped into the chowrikhang to call back the cattle.

Winter was approaching.

The dark clouds over Thungri had cast a shadow over Nimden's jolly face. The reason became apparent the next morning. The clouds churned in a roiling boil; it was accompanied by a strong wind. I remembered a description by Sarat Chandra Das of the top of the Bogto La: dark clouds scudded the skies like a herd of wild yaks, so low that it seemed he could touch them. This had been followed by heavy snowfall.

The treeline ended at Changla. All around us were boulders pulled down by avalanches in the past. Clumps of yellow grass and scruffy junipers were holding ground. No shelter, no cave or overhang, on this trail. And then a light snow began to fall like the feathers of a dead bird. We ran to an abandoned army bunker.

Since Thungri we had been seeing these tomb-shaped military bunkers on the windy slopes facing north and northwest. They had been hastily constructed by the Indian Army during the Chinese attack in 1962. Now they occasionally sheltered wayward sheep and the shepherds. The one we ran into had space for barely half a dozen men to crouch inside and stick out the muzzles of guns through narrow chinks at chest level. Empty tobacco sachets and pellets of sheep dung were strewn on the floor. Soon the muzzle holes were blocked by snow.

Nimden returned from a nearby yak-grazers' shed with grim news. Shaking off snowflakes from his cap and eyebrows, he said, 'Bad news, bad news! Snow this high on Poshing La!' He pulled both his hands to his chest.

Higher up, heavy snow had been falling continually for the past three days and had blocked the pass completely. This was really bad news because the Bailey Trail crossed Poshing La and continued along a couple of remote high-altitude villages up to the McMahon Line.

We had to take a decision. It was the end of October; officially, the winter season was yet to begin. The snowfall could be due to a temporary disturbance, not an unusual thing in this region, and might pass in a day or two. But what if it didn't? What if the winter had arrived a little prematurely? Nimden argued. We didn't have crampons or ice axes with us. The rations, too, would be depleted. Reshi, the leader of the porters and a surly man from Thembang, pointed out that the mules would starve if they were stranded in this wilderness for more than two days. They didn't want to take any chance.

'What the hell!' one of my friends shouted in despair. The whole point of our coming this far was to traverse the entire Bailey Trail inside Indian territory.

Arguments flew thick and fast, and the air inside the narrow bunker was rife with tension—not a nice thing at these heights, and in such infernal weather. We couldn't guess the short, quick exchanges that Nimden and Reshi made in their language. We couldn't even contact the agency owner at Bomdila. The Indo-China border was barely a few miles away and there was no signal on our mobile phones. While we continued to bicker in three languages, a porter lit a primus stove, broke a batch of icicles into a saucepan and emptied soup sachets into it. Nimden had remembered to bring soft fresh cheese from the yak-herders' shed.

Meanwhile the snowfall had stopped. A delicate pink light seeped in through the grim sky and gleamed over the whitened expanse. The mountains had turned out with a rare beauty. The wind, too, had ceased; it didn't feel cold. We crawled out to find the two mules standing back to back under a narrow overhang, and their driver snuggling between their haunches. He was dressed in a worn oversized jacket and yellow plastic gumboots. He also had the puzzling face of a very young boy grown prematurely old. His thick wiry hair and eyebrows were powdered with snow. I didn't learn his name, I hadn't heard anyone call out to him. It seemed as if the sole objective of his life was to remain wedged between the two living animals and draw as much warmth from them as he could. The mules stood there like stone, with the loads tied to their backs and puddles of steaming golden liquid on the fresh snow around their feet, reflecting the fading daylight.

Stranded

All the romance associated with snowfall has nothing in common with the experience of being stranded at 14,000 feet without a shelter and gear. There was no fresh snowfall at Poshing La, but we decided to abandon the trek. We set off next morning along an old army patrol route and climbed down 11 miles to the village of Chander before evening. The Bailey Trail was lost under snow, like the forgotten narrative of an empire. A hundred years after Eric Bailey had passed this region, we couldn't find any sign of it. A new nation had been built with its rubble; that, too, had grown decrepit and full of cracks.

The night before, packed like matchsticks inside the narrow bunker, with the mule driver snoring away like a field gun, we hadn't been able to catch sleep. But we weren't feeling tired. Perhaps this had got to do with the icy sense of danger at every step, the muscles and tendons at razor's edge, as we paced down the steep downward trail. By late morning most of the snow had hardened to smooth ice and our rubber-soled boots constantly lost traction. The entire path lay along open slopes, sometimes at an angle of forty-five degrees, with nothing to hold on to above the treeline. I felt a strange tickle under the soles of my feet and a faint nausea.

Nimden led us down by scratching upon the ice with a stick. The porters, shod in thin plastic gumboots and with heavy loads strapped to their backs, were hurtling down with an amazing display of agility and instinct. The mules, too, were sure-footed: they climbed down in zigzag fashion, digging away the snow with a forward movement of their front legs and placing their hind legs exactly in these spots.

The grasslands were completely snowed under, punctuated here and there by smooth boulders and the stumps of ancient trees sticking out like angry fists. These slopes had surely been under forest cover once upon a time.

'Here a big fight with Chinese army,' Nimden said in English, pointing to the ground. 'Chander Gaon Bura army man, will tell you story.'

Measureless snow, flecked with dark granite and carbonized wood. I remembered the war memorial near Tenga, and the words etched on the pink Aravalli stones. How flimsy death must have been on this endless expanse of black and grey, that no words could put on stone.

Stunted trees began to reappear at around 10,000 feet. On leafless twigs the wind-blown frost had sculpted countless tiny pointed flags.

Our spirits were low because of the aborted adventure. Nimden had sensed this and was trying to regale us with stories from his life. He narrated some of the ancient customs in their society, including a bizarre funeral ritual. Monpas in this region normally cremated the dead. But sometimes, ordained by the priests, they would cut up the dead body into one hundred and eight pieces and throw them into the river. It was somewhat like the Tibetan ritual of jhator, alms to the birds; here it was alms to the fish. Professional corpse cutters did the job. Once, when a childhood friend of Nimden had died in the village, the priest ordered a river burial to avert a curse. Incidentally, the cutter was away in the town, four days' journey by foot from the village. As they waited for him, the body began to rot. So Nimden volunteered for the job; he had watched the ritual so many times since he was a boy, it had never seemed a difficult undertaking.

And it wasn't. But since that day he lost his appetite and sleep, he even lost his senses and began attacking people for no reason. This deranged state had continued for nearly a year.

Chander sat atop a ridge at a height of 9,000 feet. A rough dirt road rarely used by army vehicles terminated here. Green chowrikhang rolled down to the forested valleys, with well-known mountains towering in the distance—Gorichen, Kangto, Nyegi Kangsang and others. But the bad weather had shut them out; we were suspended in a grey world of mist. We could only imagine how the view would be on a clear day from this perch, the edge of a ridge that jutted out like a promontory over the deep valleys.

'Thank god that this place is far away from the plains, else the British would surely have built another Darjeeling or Shimla here,' a friend quipped.

Chander was an old village of twenty-odd houses. All were Tibetan Monpas here, and cattle herders. Impressive woodwork on two or three cottages suggested that it had once been a prosperous settlement. A lime-washed chorten stood on the narrow end of the ridge. A windmill with broken wing blades stood in the middle of the village, bearing a signboard of the Department of Renewable Energy. Also a concrete school building with an abandoned look, its wooden doors and windows long rotted away. The tents were pitched on its paved courtyard.

A stout old villager in an olive-green overcoat and a sheepskin cap was helping the porters set up tents. Seeing us, he came forward and shook hands.

'Welcome to our village!' he said in English.

He was Sangay Dorjee, the Gaon Bura, about whom Nimden had told us. The Assam Service Corps logo on his overcoat, and his ramrod-straight posture and crisp manners gave away his past. But time had left its marks on his body: the twin bulges of the eyeballs sat in a nest of crow's feet with narrow slits for the eyes.

Sangay gave us bad news with a flutter of those heavy-lidded eyes. It had been snowing in the forests below for the past few days, the paths were closed. We were to take these paths to the Sangti river valley, from where a motorable road led to Dirang.

Turned back halfway through an expedition and marooned in a grim-looking village to boot, our spirits had hit rock bottom. Nimden attempted to boost it with his trademark insouciance: 'No problem. Path not open, army truck will come take Dirang.'

Sangay Dorjee nodded his head in agreement. Army patrol trucks made occasional rounds in this area, he informed. Two years back, when Chander had been cut off for nearly a month due to a heavy snowfall, the jawans had brought food and medicines.

'But not to worry, that was a rare incident. It won't take long for the snow to melt on the slopes,' Sangay assured us in English mixed with broken Hindi.

By this time a small group of elderly villagers had gathered. They endorsed Sangay with vigorous nods of their heads and rolling of tongues. Two of them fell into a passionate discussion, in their own language, on how the snow in the forests below would melt over the next few days, and which of the paths to the valley would open first. The good news was, there had been no fresh snowfall in the last twenty-four hours.

But a tearing wind was blowing ceaselessly over the bare hill top. We had to speak loudly and bring the lips close to the listeners' ears in order to be audible. The wind howled in the empty shell of the school building, rattled the broken windmill and slapped our tents. Except for us, and the half dozen old villagers, no sign of life could be detected in the village. There was a mysterious stillness, despite the movement of the wind.

We were stranded in Chander for three days. There was no fresh snowfall, but the wind hadn't let up even for a minute. Icy and sharp as a razor blade, it had searched out the chinks in the tents and clothing to lacerate the flesh. In its ceaseless roar we had lost our bearings, and even the sense of time. The pages in my diary on these three days are blank. As I look back now, it strikes me that the deft, well-oiled fashion in which I had been pinning down my experiences on the dated grids of the diary's pages, as travellers do, had become ineffectual. Those three days and nights at Chander had slipped off like an avalanche, leaving a blank, a haunting gash.

Life in the remote cattle herders' village had folded into itself, into the flimsy birdcage cottages, and had continued to swirl in slow, imperceptible movements around the lighted hearth. At night, cocooned in the sleeping bag, the wind's tireless whack against the tent walls would stir up nightmares, of Nimden slicing his friend's dead body by a blue lake, with eagles perched on crags, and Sarat Chandra, his face flaming red and covered with dark glasses, riding a pony to Samding monastery.

I'd wake up in the morning with a headache. The weather outside would be unchanged. Mustard-yellow lichens on stone would be gilded with frost like some precious inlay work. A morning village—and yet there'd be no calls of roosters, no sign of humans stirring; only a grey soupy light and ashes blowing in the air. A black mastiff bitch would lie curled up on a heap of ashes with her three pups.

A shepherd had come from a far-off village to buy one of the pups. He, too, had been stuck because of the snow. From him we learnt that the price of a well-bred mastiff could be as high as 10,000 rupees. Two full-grown dogs could easily guard a flock of two hundred sheep even without their master being around.

His name was Kachyo. A cheery young man with a dorje tattooed on his neck, a long knife in a bamboo sheath hanging on his waist, wearing jeans and faux Nike sneakers, Kachyo was a far cry from the image of a shepherd culled from storybooks. He was staying at the dog breeder's house and seemed very eager to chat with us, people from the great beyond, but the lack of a common language came in the way. Yet he would drop in at all hours of the day; he, too, had nothing to do in the lonely village. All the able-bodied men and women were staying in sheds in the middle of the chowrikhang, busy preparing butter and cheese. Winter was near and the cattle would soon be taken to the valleys. Sometimes we would see women returning with faggots or babies in baskets strapped to their backs, to attend to the household and get back to the chowrikhang again. Sometimes flocks of sheep would pass through the village, across the lanes, courtyards and homestead lands, on their way from one slope to another.

The mess tent had not been pitched because of the empty school building. The porters, too, were living inside it. In the afternoon, everyone would gather there around the blazing kerosene stove for warmth and endless cups of coffee. With the trek cut short, we had no dearth of provisions. We'd even entertain the village elders who would also drop in, the central figure among them being Sangay Dorjee. He brought regular updates on the condition of the forest paths and the whims of the snow.

The pitiless wind made it difficult to stay out in the open for long; the eyes ran and a disagreeable buzz lingered in the ear. A dry wind from Central Asia, sharpened by the snow-clad mountains, it pounced on the exposed village without a tree or a hump to protect it. In its unrelieved wheeze was borne the whimper of a lone baby dog, the one the shepherd had chosen, which had been kept isolated from its mother and siblings. The thin whimper continued throughout the night. The mother, somnolent and morose, would lie curled up near the chorten all day.

I had asked Sangay Dorjee about his experiences during the 1962 war. The villagers who had been young at the time, or had grown up hearing about it, chirped the details in a chorus. Sangay acted as the interpreter-cum-chorus leader. They described the shelling and how the mountains had trembled like the rump of a yak at the distant growl of a snow leopard, how the village had been emptied and everyone had fled into the forests below. These memories had fermented for so long that they hit them now like some potent wine. We watched the old men with a touch of amusement, because we couldn't understand a word they were saying, gesticulating with all their limbs and mimicking the report of gunshots. They resembled a bunch of excited children.

In 1962 the forests around Chander were thicker and yet to make way for extensive grazing grounds. People in these remote mountain settlements had taken cover in the forests for weeks. It was late autumn, ripe crops were standing in farm plots on the valley. The Monpas had left everything, including their cattle, and fled to the forests. After the infiltration ended, as mysteriously as it had begun, and the sound of gunfire ceased, they returned home, and the shock of their lives: the Chinese had harvested and stored the crops; they had even left fodder for the cattle.

None of us had ever heard this strange piece of information, or read about it anywhere. Seeing our incredulous faces, Sangay Dorjee smiled.

'Yes, it happened,' he said. 'The Red Army had brought farm workers with them. Their purpose was to shock the Indian government, not harm the common people or damage their properties.'

Daytime in Chander would be fleeting, enamelled with a pearly, cloud-strained light and a wind that never flagged. The unchanging view from the tent's awning would stir up memories of Alpine scenery painted on the chocolate boxes of childhood.

Throughout the day, Kachyo the shepherd would sit propped against the broken windmill, with the wind in his hair, playing Monpa songs sung by a sleek male voice on his mobile phone.

Across from the windmill, in the open terrace of a double-storeyed wooden cottage, a pale girl in a red woollen cap would frequently appear—to wash clothes, dust carpets or to chop firewood. They'd cast sidelong glances at each other, but never exchange a word.

The village had no potable water source. In the afternoon, an army of children would troop to a spring and return pulling plastic jerrycans. Years ago, there had been a spring by the village. It dried up after the jungle around it was cleared, making life harder for the villagers. But children would be children. They would snatch morsels of frolic even from the jaws of a heavy chore, rolling the empty jerrycans, flying kites made out of polythene bags and attempting a ride on the huge, shaggy, avuncular dogs of the village. Chander would briefly come alive with their merry din.

Sangay Dorjee had been making efforts to reopen the primary school. He had drafted a petition to the District Inspector of Schools and sought our help to brush it up. He would hand it over to his son during the latter's next monthly visit from Dirang.

Sangay was a widower. His two sons and a daughter lived in Dirang and Bomdila with their families. The sons were in government jobs. The one who lived in Dirang, the younger one, came every month to hand him his army pension. Sangay invited us to his cottage one afternoon and served us milk tea and sweet biscuits that he himself had baked.

It was a modest two-room cottage with a cattle shed at the back where a mithun, a domesticated gaur, was kept. The living-room was rather well-appointed with a kerosene heater, solar lamps, music system and other gadgets, but Sangay didn't make use of any of them. A village woman did the housekeeping and looked after the mithun.

'Children want me to stay with them, but the town is a crazy place. So much noise and light, and everybody running all the time. No time to stop and talk,' said Sangay. He had been born in this village and had grown up here. His only wish now was to die here and be cremated on the bank of the river Sangti, like his wife.

There was a black-and-white photograph of her upon a shelf, taken when she was young: a timid hill woman laden with jewellery against a painted backdrop of ice cream-cone mountains. Beside it was a colour photograph of Sangay Dorjee, in military uniform, looking into the camera with quiet confidence.

Sangay mostly lived in the past as there was nothing to look forward to. The jungles were being felled, the springs were drying, the high grasslands were turning brown and denuded.

'A day will come when this village, too, will need to be shifted,' he said, and reeled out the names of villages above the Sangti Valley that had been transplanted in the last twenty years. 'My only satisfaction is, I shall not be there to see that day,' he said with a smile.

Work with the Indian Army had taken Sangay Dorjee to many places. Experience had lent a refined grace to his personality, and had also set him apart from other village elders in Chander. From them, via Nimden, we came to know that Sangay Dorjee was a Brokpa, the son of a slave woman.

The Monpas had kept slaves since ancient times. They were called Brokpas. The tradition had continued in these remote regions even after Independence and the passing of antislavery laws. Brokpas, both men and women, were attached for generations to Monpa families and tended their cattle. Sometimes a Brokpa woman would have offspring sired by her master. The tradition faded away slowly, especially since the formation of NEFA and the presence of the government agencies. Sangay Dorjee of Chander was probably one of the last living members of his tribe.

Did his life originate in a grazer's shed in the middle of a desolate chowrikhang? I would never know. I had seen an old battered yak bell in his room; it was kept on a shelf above the photographs of him and his wife, beside a framed colour print of the fourteenth Dalai Lama.

I wanted to know where I could buy such a bell.

'You can get them in the bazaars in Tawang and Bomdila, but the quality of metal is poor,' Sangay said. 'These old ones are made of a hard alloy that the traders used to bring from Tibet. They have stopped coming after the War.'

The yak bell in Sangay Dorjee's cottage didn't ring anymore, the clapper was missing. But perhaps it continued to jingle in his memories. Only I couldn't hear it.

I heard other sounds. All night long, the wind slapping the tent walls and wheezing through the mounds of faggots continued to trouble sleep like a marching army. I woke up in a daze and remembered something Norbu had told me many years ago, about a liminal state between life and death in the cycle of rebirth, as described in some Tibetan Buddhist texts. It was not easy to imagine that state. But waking into an extraordinary silence, with a strange hollowness in the head, I felt it could perhaps be something like this.

A couple of seconds passed before I realized that the wind

had ceased. A faint shadow of the chorten was cast on the blue tent wall. I crept outside to find the delicate rays of the morning sun coming in from under the woolly sheet of clouds overhead. In the distant horizon, set against a narrow strip of opalescent sky, stood the snow-covered ranges. Before me, around the chorten, a herd of sheep lay still like flakes of snow.

I was about to call out to my sleeping friends, but I stopped. A bird was calling in a thin monotone from a chink in the chorten wall. It was a tiny bird, with reddish-green plumage that perfectly camouflaged it against the moss-covered basalt: a laughing thrush.

That day we trekked 4,000 feet down slushy forest paths to the Sangti Valley. Next morning a Tata Sumo came from Dirang to collect us.

A Dead Weight

Sangay Dorjee gave me a yak's bell as a farewell gift the day we left Chander. It was a replica of the one I had seen in his cottage, but it was in better shape, and had a wooden clapper inside. As I look back now on those three days we spent in Chander, I find with some uneasiness that I really don't have much memory of it. I have read about people suffering from temporary loss of memory at high altitudes; but Chander was only 9,000 feet. I don't have anything with me of those three days, except certain images and sensations.

And this yak bell that now sits on my bookshelf.

All five of us suffered bouts of depression in that little yak-herders' village on the bare mountaintop. This manifested itself in binge drinking, frayed tempers and pointless spats. The absence of comfort inside the tents had suddenly become an issue. Minor oddities of behaviour, which in other times were a source of much humour and had enlivened our trips together, became magnified into points of friction. We had even grown suspicious of each other, sometimes rather comically so. These were so flimsy that by the time we had reached Dirang, none of us could remember any of it. It all seemed like a bad dream we had dreamed together.

A dreary, endless dream from which we'd never wake up, it had seemed. The world had shrunk inside a tent made of interminable grey fog, and in the murky light that penetrated it, a grey miniature village stood stark and deadly still. But that light, too, would go off prematurely and night would fall when it was only afternoon.

It was the third and last day of our enforced stay in Chander. At around 3 p.m.—daylight was to fade in half an hour—I went alone to Sangay Dorjee's cottage at the far end of the village, on the edge of a rocky incline dotted with clumps of grass. Not a soul was out in the open. Smoke coming out from a couple cottage eaves indicated the presence of life inside. The wind had a shifting, fitful quality about it. Plastic wrappers and bits of ash gusted up in the air. The two little mastiff pups were chasing them around. Their mother couldn't be seen. The whimper of their quarantined sibling had ceased.

I would learn later that the shepherd had returned to his village with it. The platform of the windmill had become desolate. The girl with the red cap, too, had become less busy with household chores.

I found Sangay inside the cow shed, just back from the forest below with a mound of wild leaves and creepers, fodder for the mithun. He had on a coarse gunny cloak tied to his neck, blue plastic gumboots and the piquant smell of vegetation about him. He motioned me inside the cottage with a broad smile and quickly changed to his olive green service jacket and the sheepskin cap.

Snow had begun to melt in the forest and the paths would soon open, Sangay told me. He lit the kerosene room heater and poured warm chhang from a kettle into two small porcelain bowls. I had a little brandy in my hip flask. The wind had found a way through the tin roof and the bamboo matting on the ceiling fluttered like a flock of large birds trying to take wing.

'No, I didn't fight in the '62 war,' Sangay admitted. 'That time I was posted at the command headquarters in Tezpur. Our duty was to send supplies to the forward lines, and stock up ration and fuel.'

By that time he had been working in the Assam Rifles for ten years, and he loved his job. The tough life of a jawan was nothing compared to that of a yak-herder. When he was still a young boy, every day Sangay had to patrol a vast chowrikhang spread over two contiguous spurs, look after the cattle and attend to their various ailments, milk them and prepare cheese and butter. At the end of a hard day's work, all he received from his Monpa owner was leftover food and a corner in the cattle shed to sleep at night.

Meanwhile, India had become independent. It had taken more than a year for the news to reach these remote NEFA settlements.

'In those days, there were no paths connecting our villages. I cannot tell you how cut-off we were. If someone came on a visit from Dirang, everyone in the village would leave whatever he was doing and rush to see the person.'

When Sangay was a child, his mother would often tell him about a big town beyond the mountains. It was by the bank of a river. One day he fled with a group of Tibetan cannabis sellers. They walked for eight days and crossed a number of mountains, until they reached a town on the plains.

Sangay had never seen a town before. He was horrified. Everywhere there were heaps of rubble and wood, cracked and fallen houses, and smoke rising from deep fissures in the earth. It was a nightmare town.

The Assam earthquake of 1950 had struck a few weeks earlier.

Assam Rifles was recruiting men for reconstruction work. Sangay Dorjee got the job of a Sawar. He was seventeen. When the war with China broke out, he had already become a Lance Naik.

'The Chinese attacked on the 20th of October. But not in the NEFA. The battle in NEFA didn't begin before the middle of November. They captured Bomdila on the 18th. Next day, news reached us that the Red Army had advanced into the plains and were on their way to Tezpur. Orders came from the Guwahati headquarters to leave post immediately. Chaos broke out as people saw army convoys leaving the town. The air was thick with rumours. The Chinese had cut off the telephone lines. Only the radio was working. We learnt one morning that there had been an attempt to torch the oil refinery at Noonmatti. That day, around noon, it aired Punditji's shattering speech. My heart goes out to the people of Assam, he had said.

'And then terror swept like a forest fire. There was a mad scramble to leave the town. The planters were the first to flee.

'There was a tea garden manager's bungalow close to our barracks. The sahib manager owned five bulldogs. He herded his family into a jeep, loaded all the valuables and drove off to Guwahati, and flew to Calcutta in a chartered plane. Before he left, he shot all the five dogs himself. Next day the collector sahib left the town.

'An order had been issued to burn all currency notes in banks and the treasury. People cleared out of Tezpur before nightfall. They grabbed whatever mode of transport they could find—trucks, buses, oxcarts, cycles, even on foot. The East Bengali laskars plied the boats of the steamship company on Brahmaputra all day long. They were taking people to the other bank of the river in exchange for cash and jewellery. Even women. But they too didn't return after dark. The hapless people went to take cover inside the tea gardens.

'Only three of us from our unit had stayed back—Subedar Thapa, Lance Naik Thatar and I. Others had fled.

'It was a completely deserted town by night, and so quiet. Only the street dogs were barking in the dark. There was no electricity. At Kasaibazaar we saw a well-bred race horse that somebody had abandoned. Tezpur had a big racecourse, you know. Burnt currency notes drifted about everywhere. We saw a group of mad men who had slipped out of the sanatorium.

'The moon rose at midnight. We didn't have a morsel of food since morning, our legs felt heavy like lead with all the walking. We entered the Planters' Club. Nobody was inside. We went to the cellar and found it stocked up with canned food and crates of beer. In the lounge, moon beams had entered through the skylight and cast huge shadows of bison heads on the walls. Subedar Thapa turned on Radio Peking. Zhou En Lai was declaring a ceasefire. It was the 21st of November.'

Sangay paused. His heavy-lidded eyes were fixed upon the empty bowl in his hand. He looked tired.

But stray skirmishes had continued even after the declaration of the ceasefire. It had taken several days for the news to reach the remote regions. A team of men from the Assam Rifles were sent to the mountains. Sangay Dorjee was selected in that team. They were sent to Poshing La pass, where there had been a heavy gunfight. Sangay knew the area well, he had grazed yaks in the pastureland below when he was a boy.

Twelve years after his escape from Chander, he saw again the mountains, springs and the trees that he had known since childhood. Nothing appeared to have changed, only the villages were completely empty. It was December, the upper reaches were under heavy snow. But they had been given proper clothing, ice axes, boots fitted with crampons, and large quantities of white canvas. They were not told what the last item was for. Sangay had thought the team was being sent to announce the ceasefire to the ignorant armies clashing in the snow, that the bales of white canvas had been given to them to make peace flags. But on reaching Poshing La they learnt that they were to collect the dead men. The battle had ceased a month earlier, the bodies of their fellow jawans were still lying under the snow.

'All the boys were from the Sikh Light Infantry Division,' Sangay said slowly. 'Most had died of freezing cold after receiving minor bullet wounds. They only had cotton clothes and canvas shoes on them. After so many weeks, the bodies were still fresh. It seemed as if they had died moments ago. Tall, healthy men, and so young—all in their early teens and twenties. A few years younger than I was then. But now, when I look back, I think they were like my grandchildren. They had been born and had grown up in the flat green plains of north India, in villages by the rivers. They had to come this far, to these lonely mountains, only to die.'

It took them five days to recover all the bodies from under the snow and prepare them to take back to the outpost in Bomdila. They had to make biers with their rifles to carry them down steep mountain slopes to the trucks. Some of the bodies were found at such sheer heights that they had to tie them on their backs and rappel down the precipices on ropes.

The snow had melted, the cycle of seasons had turned, the mountain slopes had come back to life with the shimmering blue poppies and the chimes of yaks' bells. Sangay had retired from service and returned to his village. These were distant memories that lay buried in his mind, only to well up on a grey windy afternoon, before a persistent visitor. But sometimes when he trudged up from the forest carrying mounds of fodder to his lonely cottage, he was ambushed by the memory of a dead weight on his back, of pairs of eyes, open and undefiled, under glassy sheets of ice inlaid with blood.

Bibliography

Works I Have Consulted and a List for Further Reading

'Report of the Death of Mr. Csoma de Koros, made to G.A. Bushby, Esq., Officiating secretary, Political Department, from A. Campbell, Esq., Superintendent, Darjeeling and Communicated to the Society', *Journal of the Asiatic Society of Bengal*, vol. 11, 1842.

'Report on Explorations in Sikkim, Bhutan and Tibet', *Records of the Survey of India*, 1889.

'The Journals of Major James Rennel', *The Asiatic Society of Bengal*, vol iii, Calcutta, 1910.

Bailey, Frederick Marshman, 'Correspondence. The Tsangpo'. Meetings of the Royal Geographic Society, Session 1912–13.

Bailey, Frederick Marshman, 'Exploration on the Tsangpo or Upper Brahmaputra', *The Geographical Journal*, October 1914.

Bailey, Frederick Marshman. 'Note on a Portion of the Tsangpo', *The Geographical Journal*, vol. 66, no. 6, 1925.

Bailey, Frederick Marshman. 'The Story of Kintup', *The Geographical Journal*, vol. 15, 1943.

Bailey, Frederick Marshman. *No Passport to Tibet.* London: Rupert Hart-Davis, 1957.

Candler, Edmund. *The Unveiling of Lhasa.* London: Edward Arnold & Company, 1905.

Croner, Don. *Eccentric Hungarian Wanderer—Scholar Csoma de Körös and the Legend of Shambhala.* Anchorage, AK: Polar Star Publishing, 2016.

Das, Baboo Sarat Chandra Das. 'Contributions on the Religion, History, &c, of Tibet: Rise and Progress of Jîn Or Buddhism in

China', *Journal of the Asiatic Society of Bengal*, volume L, issue III, 1881.

Das, Sarat Chandra Das. *Autobiography—Narratives of the Incidents of My Early Life*. Calcutta: Indian Studies, 1969.

Das, Sarat Chandra. *A Journey to Lhasa and Central Tibet*. London: John Murray, 1902.

David-Néel, Alexandra. *Magic and Mystery in Tibet*, New York: Dover Publications, 1929.

Fox, Edward. *The Hungarian Who Walked to Heaven-Alexander Csoma De Koros-1784-1842*. London: Short Books, 2001.

Grothmann, Kerstin. 'Population History and Identity in the Hidden Land of Pemako', *Journal of Bhutan Studies*, vol. 26, 2010.

Narratives of the Mission of George Bogle to Tibet, and of the Journey of Thomas Manning to Lhasa, Clements R. Markham, London, 1876.

Oakes, G.F.T. 'Note in Vindication of Kinthup', *Records of the Survey of India*, vol. 7, 1913–14.

Rennel, James. *A Memoir upon the Maps of Bengal, Constructed from 1764 Onwards*. Calcutta: The Bengal Secretariat Book Depot, 1914.

Ward, Frank Kingdon. *Adventures in Furthest Tibet: The Riddle of the Tsangpo Gorges*. London: Edward Arnold & Company, 1926.

Younghusband, Francis. *Memorandum on Our Relations with Tibet, Both Past and Present, Together with a Forecast of the Future Development of Our Policy in That Region*. Shimla, 1903.